CW00839246

WORLD
WAR I
POETRY

WORLD WAR I POETRY

A Collection of Haunting Verses from the Great War

Introduction by Dr Spencer Jones

SIRIUS

Picture Credits

Getty Images: /Culture Club: 25; /Galerie Bilderwelt: 33; /Past Pix: 45; /Photo 12: 48; Topical Press Agency/stringer: 59; /FPG: 62–63; /IWM: 74–75; /Universal History archive: 91; /Hulton Deutsch: 104;

Shutterstock: 11, 12–13, 17, 20–21, 30, 36, 46, 50, 52, 56–57, 61, 70–71, 80–81, 82–83, 84, 86–87, 95, 97, 98–99, 101, 102–03, 106–07, 109, 116–17, 118, 119, 123, 129, 131, 132–33, 135, 137, 138–39, 140, 141, 142, 148–49, 155

SIRIUS

This edition published in 2017 by Sirius Publishing, a division of Arcturus Publishing Limited,
26/27 Bickels Yard, 151–153 Bermondsey Street,
London SE1 3HA

Copyright © Arcturus Holdings Limited
Pages 50–53: Copyright Siegfried Sassoon by kind permission of the Estate of George Sassoon.
Pages 108–110: Quotations from Vera Brittain are included by permission of Mark Bostridge and T. J. Brittain-Catlin, Literary Executors for the Estate of Vera Brittain 1970.
Pages 120–121: The Driver Gunner is published by permission of the translator, Ian Higgins, and publisher, Saxon Books.
Page 126: To A Lark in War-Time was translated by Edith Abercrombie Snow/Published by Princeton University Press, 1945

ISBN: 978-1-78428-907-2
AD005707UK

Printed in China

Contents

Introduction

William Wordsworth believed that 'all good poetry is the spontaneous overflow of powerful feelings'. It is perhaps little wonder that war, with all its tremendous and conflicting emotions, has so often proved a source of inspiration for poets. From Homer's Illiad to Lord Tennyson's The Charge of the Light Brigade and beyond, images of war have produced some of history's most enduring poetry.

Yet even in this rich field, there is something exceptional about the poetry of World War I. Such is the cultural and literary importance of the poetry from this conflict that the term "war poets" has become synonymous with the trenches of 1914–18. This mirrors the uniqueness of the fighting. At the time, it was the largest, bloodiest and most intensely fought war in human history. The scale of the conflict meant that entire nations were mobilized. Britain raised the largest army in its history, filling the ranks first with volunteers, and later with conscripts. This unprecedented level of participation meant that men and women were suddenly exposed to a new way of life. Previous social norms were abandoned as women took on jobs formerly undertaken by males, whilst men who had never travelled beyond their home village suddenly found themselves in the fields of France or on the beaches of Gallipoli.

For soldiers in the front line, the experience was disorientating. War had been portrayed in a romantic light before the conflict, but troops soon discovered that the fighting of World War I bore no resemblance to the heroic image beloved by artists. Combat was appallingly violent. The machine technology of the early 20th century was harnessed and brought to bear against flesh and bone. Individuals were powerless against the overwhelming weight of bullets, shrapnel and poison gas that swept the battlefields. The Germans gave it a word: materialschlacht or 'the battle of material'. The fighting mutilated bodies and damaged minds. The previously unknown phenomenon of 'shell shock', now known as post-traumatic stress disorder, was first observed during the war.

The sheer novelty of the conditions made it difficult for participants to express the sights and sounds they faced. In an era when photography and film were in their infancy and unable to capture the reality of battle, poetry offered a penetrating insight into the realities of this new form of warfare. The best poems allow the reader to go beyond the sepia photographs and, for a moment, experience the war in full colour. The vivid imagery in the most famous of World War I poems leaves a profound impression. Lines such as 'Of poisonous fumes that scorched the night / With their sulphurous demon danks' in William Wilfred Campbell's 'Langemark at Ypres' or 'Manic Earth! Howling and flying' as it is churned by artillery fire in Isaac Rosenberg's 'Dead Man's Dump' serve to remind the reader that the war was neither colourless nor silent.

The poetry of World War I has created a lasting image of horror and futility in the public conscious. Yet the motivations of war poets were varied and their experiences could often be ambiguous. War itself is a complex interplay of conflicting emotions: despair, misery, terror, comradeship, exhilaration, and even glory. This emotional ambiguity is reflected in much of the best war poetry. Perhaps the most famous example is found in John McCrae's *In Flanders Fields*. The first two verses are often quoted as an example of anti-war poetry, whilst the bellicose third verse is marginalized or even ignored.

War poetry underwent a noticeable change as the war dragged on. In an unconscious echo of the work of William Blake, innocence gave way to experience. The jingoist appeals of Jessie Pope and the romantic sacrifice extoled by Rupert Brooke found an audience in the late summer of 1914. But the mood changed as the reality of war became apparent. The all-volunteer British Army of 1914–15 fought bravely and suffered terribly, but could not secure victory. Conscription was introduced in 1916 to ensure sufficient men for the great Allied offensive at the Battle of the Somme. More British casualties were suffered in the five months of this battle than in the previous two years combined, yet it failed to breach the German lines. In 1917, came the Third Battle of Ypres; a mud-stricken, attritional nightmare that became an emblem of the war itself. After three years of war, the hopeful spirit of 1914 was long gone. War poetry assumed a markedly darker tone in 1917–18, adopting themes of frustration, disenchantment and even despair.

The famous poems of these latter years of the war are often cited as representing the experience of the whole British Army. This is misleading. Many published war poets were officers of the educated class who found the deprived conditions of trench life and the roar of battle utterly alien. But for private soldiers drawn from noisome inner city slums and accustomed to work in heavy industry, the transition was rather different. Furthermore, in an army of millions, there was no such thing as a universal experience. What war poetry does offer is a snapshot into the mind of the poet at that moment in time. It is colourful, powerful, moving and thought-provoking. It provides an injection of raw emotion into a conflict that continues to fascinate us a century later. The remarkable endurance of the poetry of World War I is testament to its merit and importance. It deserves to be read, studied and enjoyed for many decades to come.

Dr Spencer Jones
Senior Lecturer in Armed Forces and War Studies
University of Wolverhampton

Into Battle

The naked earth is warm with Spring,
        And with green grass and bursting trees
Leans to the sun's gaze glorying,
And quivers in the sunny breeze;
And life is Colour and Warmth and Light,
And a striving evermore for these;
And he is dead who will not fight;
And who dies fighting has increase.

The fighting man shall from the sun
Take warmth, and life from glowing earth;
Speed with the light-foot winds to run,
And with the trees to newer birth;
And find, when fighting shall be done,
Great rest, and fullness after dearth.

All the bright company of Heaven
Hold him in their bright comradeship,
The Dog-star, and the Sisters Seven,
Orion's belt and sworded hip:

The woodland trees that stand together,
They stand to him each one a friend;
They gently speak in the windy weather;
They guide to valley and ridge's end.

The kestrel hovering by day,
And the little owls that call by night,
Bid him be swift and keen as they,
As keen of ear, as swift of sight.

The blackbird sings to him: 'Brother, brother,
    If this be the last song you shall sing,
  Sing well, for you may not sing another;
Brother, sing.'

In dreary doubtful waiting hours,
Before the brazen frenzy starts,
The horses show him nobler powers;
O patient eyes, courageous hearts!

And when the burning moment breaks,
And all things else are out of mind,
And only joy of battle takes
Him by the throat and makes him blind,

Through joy and blindness he shall know,
Not caring much to know, that still
Nor lead nor steel shall reach him, so
That it be not the Destined Will.

The thundering line of battle stands,
And in the air death moans and sings;
But Day shall clasp him with strong hands,
And Night shall fold him in soft wings.

Julian Grenfell

The Second Coming

Turning and turning in widening gyre
    The falcon cannot hear the falconer;
    Things fall apart; the centre cannot hold;
Mere anarchy is loosed upon the world,
The blood-dimmed tide is loosed, and everywhere
The ceremony of innocence is drowned;
The best lack all conviction, while the worst
Are full of passionate intensity.

Surely some revelation is at hand;
Surely the Second Coming is at hand.
The Second Coming! Hardly are those words out
When a vast image out of *Spiritus Mundi*
Troubles my sight: somewhere in sands of the desert
A shape with lion body and the head of a man,
A gaze blank and pitiless as the sun,
Is moving its slow thighs, while all about it
Reel shadows of the indignant desert birds.
The darkness drops again; but now I know
That twenty centuries of stony sleep
Were vexed to nightmare by a rocking cradle,
And what rough beast, its hour come round at last,
Slouches towards Bethlehem to be born?

W. B. Yeats

On Being Asked for a War Poem

I think it better that in times like these
A poet's mouth be silent, for in truth
We have no gift to set a statesman right;
He has had enough of meddling who can please
A young girl in the indolence of her youth,
Or an old man upon a winter's night.

W. B. Yeats

I. Peace

Now, God be thanked Who has matched us with His hour,
    And caught our youth, and wakened us from sleeping!
With hand made sure, clear eye, and sharpened power,
To turn, as swimmers into cleanness leaping,
Glad from a world grown old and cold and weary;
Leave the sick hearts that honor could not move,
And half-men, and their dirty songs and dreary,
And all the little emptiness of love!

Oh! we, who have known shame, we have found release there,
Where there's no ill, no grief, but sleep has mending,
Naught broken save this body, lost but breath;
Nothing to shake the laughing heart's long peace there,
But only agony, and that has ending;
And the worst friend and enemy is but Death.

Rupert Brooke

II. Safety

Dear! of all happy in the hour, most blest
He who has found our hid security,
Assured in the dark tides of the world that rest,
And heard our word, 'Who is so safe as we?'
We have found safety with all things undying,
The winds, and morning, tears of men and mirth,
The deep night, and birds singing, and clouds flying,
And sleep, and freedom, and the autumnal earth.
We have built a house that is not for Time's throwing.
We have gained a peace unshaken by pain for ever.
War knows no power. Safe shall be my going,
Secretly armed against all death's endeavour;
Safe though all safety's lost; safe where men fall;
And if these poor limbs die, safest of all.

Rupert Brooke

III. The Dead

BLOW out, you bugles, over the rich Dead!
There's none of these so lonely and poor of old,
But, dying, has made us rarer gifts than gold.
These laid the world away; poured out the red
Sweet wine of youth; gave up the years to be
Of work and joy, and that unhoped serene,
That men call age; and those who would have been,
Their sons, they gave, their immortality.

Blow, bugles, blow! They brought us, for our dearth,
Holiness, lacked so long, and Love, and Pain.
Honour has come back, as a king, to earth,
And paid his subjects with a royal wage;
And Nobleness walks in our ways again;
And we have come into our heritage.

Rupert Brooke

IV. The Dead

These hearts were woven of human joys and cares,
  Washed marvellously with sorrow, swift to mirth.
The years had given them kindness. Dawn was theirs,
And sunset, and the colours of the earth.
These had seen movement, and heard music; known
Slumber and waking; loved; gone proudly friended;
Felt the quick stir of wonder; sat alone;
Touched flowers and furs and cheeks. All this is ended.

There are waters blown by changing winds to laughter
And lit by the rich skies, all day. And after,
Frost, with a gesture, stays the waves that dance
And wandering loveliness. He leaves a white
Unbroken glory, a gathered radiance,
A width, a shining peace, under the night.

Rupert Brooke

V. The Soldier

If I should die, think only this of me:
That there's some corner of a foreign field
That is for ever England. There shall be
In that rich earth a richer dust concealed;
A dust whom England bore, shaped, made aware,
Gave, once, her flowers to love, her ways to roam;
A body of England's, breathing English air,
Washed by the rivers, blest by suns of home.

And think, this heart, all evil shed away,
A pulse in the eternal mind, no less
Gives somewhere back the thoughts by England given;
Her sights and sounds; dreams happy as her day;
And laughter, learnt of friends; and gentleness,
In hearts at peace, under an English heaven.

Rupert Brooke

The Night Patrol

Over the top! The wire's thin here, unbarbed
 Plain rusty coils, not staked, and low enough:
Full of old tins, though – 'When you're through, all three,
Aim quarter left for fifty yards or so,
Then straight for that new piece of German wire;
See if it's thick, and listen for a while
For sounds of working; don't run any risks;
About an hour; now, over!'
                                    And we placed
Our hands on the topmost sand-bags, leapt, and stood
A second with curved backs, then crept to the wire,
Wormed ourselves tinkling through, glanced back, and dropped.
The sodden ground was splashed with shallow pools,
And tufts of crackling cornstalks, two years old,
No man had reaped, and patches of spring grass.
Half-seen, as rose and sank the flares, were strewn
The wrecks of our attack: the bandoliers,
Packs, rifles, bayonets, belts, and haversacks,
Shell fragments, and the huge whole forms of shells
Shot fruitlessly – and everywhere the dead.
Only the dead were always present – present
As a vile sickly smell of rottenness;
The rustling stubble and the early grass,
The slimy pools – the dead men stank through all,
Pungent and sharp; as bodies loomed before,
And as we passed, they stank: then dulled away
To that vague fœtor, all encompassing,
Infecting earth and air. They lay, all clothed,
Each in some new and piteous attitude

That we well marked to guide us back: as he,
Outside our wire, that lay on his back and crossed
His legs Crusader-wise; I smiled at that,
And thought on Elia and his Temple Church.
From him, at quarter left, lay a small corpse,
Down in a hollow, huddled as in a bed,
That one of us put his hand on unawares.
Next was a bunch of half a dozen men
All blown to bits, an archipelago
Of corrupt fragments, vexing to us three,
Who had no light to see by, save the flares.
On such a trail, so lit, for ninety yards
We crawled on belly and elbows, till we saw,
Instead of lumpish dead before our eyes,
The stakes and crosslines of the German wire.
We lay in shelter of the last dead man,
Ourselves as dead, and heard their shovels ring
Turning the earth, then talk and cough at times.
A sentry fired and a machine-gun spat;
They shot a flare above us, when it fell
And spluttered out in the pools of No Man's Land,
We turned and crawled past the remembered dead:
Past him and him, and them and him, until,
For he lay some way apart, we caught the scent
Of the Crusader and slid past his legs,
And through the wire and home, and got our rum.

Arthur Graeme West

God! How I Hate You, You Young Cheerful Men

God! How I hate you, you young cheerful men,
Whose pious poetry blossoms on your graves
As soon as you are in them, nurtured up
By the salt of your corruption, and the tears
Of mothers, local vicars, college deans,
And flanked by prefaces and photographs
From all you minor poet friends – the fools –
Who paint their sentimental elegies
Where sure, no angel treads; and, living, share
The dead's brief immortality

                              Oh Christ!
To think that one could spread the ductile wax
Of his fluid youth to Oxford's glowing fires
And take her seal so ill! Hark how one chants –
'Oh happy to have lived these epic days' –
'These epic days'! And he'd been to France,
And seen the trenches, glimpsed the huddled dead
In the periscope, hung in the rusting wire:
Choked by their sickly fœtor, day and night
Blown down his throat: stumbled through ruined hearths,
Proved all that muddy brown monotony,
Where blood's the only coloured thing. Perhaps
Had seen a man killed, a sentry shot at night,
Hunched as he fell, his feet on the firing-step,
His neck against the back slope of the trench,
And the rest doubled up between, his head
Smashed like and egg-shell, and the warm grey brain
Spattered all bloody on the parados:

Had flashed a torch on his face, and known his friend,
Shot, breathing hardly, in ten minutes – gone!
Yet still God's in His heaven, all is right
In the best possible of worlds. The woe,
Even His scaled eyes must see, is partial, only
A seeming woe, we cannot understand.
God loves us, God looks down on this our strife
And smiles in pity, blows a pipe at times
And calls some warriors home. We do not die,
God would not let us, He is too 'intense',
Too 'passionate', a whole day sorrows He
Because a grass-blade dies. How rare life is!
On earth, the love and fellowship of men,
Men sternly banded: banded for what end?
Banded to maim and kill their fellow men –
For even Huns are men. In heaven above
A genial umpire, a good judge of sport,
Won't let us hurt each other! Let's rejoice
God keeps us faithful, pens us still in fold.
Ah, what a faith is ours (almost, it seems,
Large as a mustard-seed) – we trust and trust,
Nothing can shake us! Ah, how good God is
To suffer us be born just now, when youth
That else would rust, can slake his blade in gore,
Where very God Himself does seem to walk
The bloody fields of Flanders He so loves!

Arthur Graeme West

In October 1914

I

GLOOM!
An October like November;
August a hundred thousand hours,
And all September,
A hundred thousand, dragging sunlit days,
And half October like a thousand years . . .
And doom!
That then was Antwerp. . .
                    In the name of God,
How could they do it?
Those souls that usually dived
Into the dirty caverns of mines;
Who usually hived
In whitened hovels; under ragged poplars;
Who dragged muddy shovels, over the grassy mud,
Lumbering to work over the greasy sods. . .
Those men there, with the appearance of clods
Were the bravest men that a usually listless priest of God
Ever shrived. . .
And it is not for us to make them an anthem.
If we found words there would come no wind that
    would fan them
To a tune that the trumpets might blow it,
Shrill through the heaven that's ours or yet Allah's,
Or the wide halls of any Valhallas.
We can make no such anthem. So that all that is ours
For inditing in sonnets, pantoums, elegiacs, or lays
Is this:
'In the name of God, how could they do it?'

II

For there is no new thing under the sun,
Only this uncomely man with a smoking gun
In the gloom. . .
What the devil will he gain by it?
Digging a hole in the mud and standing all day in the
    rain by it
Waiting his doom;
The sharp blow, the swift outpouring of the blood,
Till the trench of gray mud
Is turned to a brown purple drain by it.
Well, there have been scars
Won in many wars . . .

Punic,
Lacedæmonian, wars of Napoleon, wars for faith, wars
   for honour, for love, for possession,
But this Belgian man in his ugly tunic,
His ugly round cap, shooting on, in a sort of obsession,
Overspreading his miserable land,
Standing with his wet gun in his hand . . .
Doom!
He finds that in a sudden scrimmage,
And lies, an unsightly lump on the sodden grass . . .
An image that shall take long to pass!

III

For the white-limbed heroes of Hellas ride by upon their
   horses
Forever through our brains.
The heroes of Cressy ride by upon their stallions;
And battalions and battalions and battalion —
The Old Guard, the Young Guard, the men of Minden
   and of Waterloo,
Pass, for ever staunch,
Stand, for ever true;
And the small man with the large paunch,
And the gray coat, and the large hat, and the hands
   behind the back,
Watches them pass
In our minds for ever . . .
But that clutter of sodden corses
On the sodden Belgian grass —
That is a strange new beauty.

IV

With no especial legends of marchings or triumphs or
    duty,
Assuredly that is the way of it,
The way of beauty . . .
And that is the highest word you can find to say of it.
For you cannot praise it with words
Compounded of lyres and swords,
But the thought of the gloom and the rain
And the ugly coated figure, standing beside a drain,
Shall eat itself into your brain:
And you will say of all heroes, 'They fought like the
    Belgians!'
And you will say: 'He wrought like a Belgian his fate out
    of gloom.'
And you will say: 'He bought like a Belgian his doom.'
And that shall be an honourable name;
'Belgian' shall be an honourable word;
As honourable as the fame of the sword,
As honourable as the mention of the many-chorded lyre,
And his old coat shall seem as beautiful as the fabrics
    woven in Tyre.

V

And what in the world did they bear it for?
I don't know.
And what in the world did they dare it for?
Perhaps that is not for the likes of me to understand.
They could very well have watched a hundred legions go
Over their fields and between their cities
Down into more southerly regions.

They could very well have let the legions pass through
    their woods,
And have kept their lives and their wives and their
    children and cattle and goods.
I don't understand.
Was it just love of their land?
Oh, poor dears!
Can any man so love his land?
Give them a thousand thousand pities
And rivers and rivers of tears
To wash off the blood from the cities of Flanders.

VI

This is Charing Cross;
It is midnight;
There is a great crowd
And no light.
A great crowd, all black that hardly whispers aloud.
Surely, that is a dead woman – a dead mother!
She has a dead face;
She is dressed all in black;
She wanders to the bookstall and back,
At the back of the crowd;
And back again and again back,
She sways and wanders.

This is Charing Cross;
It is one o'clock.
There is still a great cloud, and very little light;
Immense shafts of shadows over the black crowd
That hardly whispers aloud. . .

And now! . . That is another dead mother,
And there is another and another and another. . .
And little children, all in black,
All with dead faces, waiting in all the waiting-places,
Wandering from the doors of the waiting-room
In the dim gloom.
These are the women of Flanders.
They await the lost.
They await the lost that shall never leave the dock;
They await the lost that shall never again come by the
    train
To the embraces of all these women with dead faces;
They await the lost who lie dead in trench and barrier
    and foss,
In the dark of the night.
This is Charing Cross; it is past one of the clock;
There is very little light.

There is so much pain.

L'Envoi
And it was for this that they endured this gloom;
This October like November,
That August like a hundred thousand hours,
And that September,
A hundred thousand dragging sunlit days,
And half October like a thousand years. . .
Oh, poor dears!

Ford Madox Ford

Before Action

By all the glories of the day
  And the cool evening's benison:
By that last sunset touch that lay
Upon the hills when day was done:
By beauty lavishly outpoured
And blessings carelessly received,
By all the days that I have lived
Make me a soldier, Lord.

By all of all man's hopes and fears,
And all the wonders poets sing,
The laughter of unclouded years,
And every sad and lovely thing;
By the romantic ages stored
With high endeavour that was his,
By all his mad catastrophes
Make me a man, O Lord.

I, that on my familiar hill
Saw with uncomprehending eyes
A hundred of thy sunsets spill
Their fresh and sanguine sacrifice,
Ere the sun swings his noonday sword
Must say good-bye to all of this: –
By all delights that I shall miss,
Help me to die, O Lord.

W. N. Hodgson

Release

A leaping wind from England,
The skies without a stain,
Clean cut against the morning
Slim poplars after rain,
The foolish noise of sparrows
And starlings in a wood –
After the grime of battle
We know that these are good.

Death whining down from heaven,
Death roaring from the ground,
Death stinking in the nostril,
Death shrill in every sound,
Doubting we charged and conquered –
Hopeless we struck and stood;
Now when the fight is ended
We know that it was good.

We that have seen the strongest
Cry like a beaten child,
The sanest eyes unholy,
The cleanest hands defiled,
We that have known the heart-blood
Less than the lees of wine,
We that have seen men broken,
We know that man is divine.

W. N. Hodgson

No!

By bridge and battery, town and trench,
They're fighting with bull-dog pluck;
Not one, from Tommy to General French,
Is down upon his luck.
There are some who stand and some who fall,
But how does the chorus go
That echoing chant in the hearts of all?
'Are we downhearted? NO!'
There's Jack, God bless him, upon the foam,
His isn't an easy task,
To strike for England, to strike right home,
So much, no more, does he ask.
On the dreadnought's deck where the big guns bark,
Or in quiet depths below
The salt wind wafts us a chantey. Hark !
'Are we downhearted? NO!'

And what of the girl who is left behind,
And the wife who misses her mate?
Oh, well, we've got our business to mind
Though it's only to watch and wait.
So we'll take what comes with a gallant heart
As we busily knit and sew,
Trying, God help us, to do our part,
'Are we downhearted? NO!

Jessie Pope

Marching to Germany

Swing along together, lads; we'll have a little song,
Kits won't be so heavy and the way won't be so long.
We're goin' to cook 'the Sossiges,' to cook 'em hot and
    strong
While we go marching to Germany.

Chorus

Hurrah, hurrah, for Berlin on the Spree!
Hurrah, hurrah, there's 'Sossiges' for tea!
We're out to catch the Kaiser and bring him to his knee
While we go marching to Germany.

How the girls all love us as they see us marching by!
Some of them are saucy ones, and some of them are shy.
Guess they know we're cold and wet to keep them warm
    and dry
While we go marching to Germany.

Chorus

What about the slacker chaps, who look before they leap?
Lads who like to save their skins and have their proper sleep
Let them put on petticoats and feel a little cheap,
While we go marching to Germany.

Chorus

Britain's little Army can be swept away like fluff;
That's the Kaiser's fairy tale ice we'll give the beggars
    snuff;
Rattle 'em and bustle 'em, and make 'em shout 'Enough!'
While we go marching to Germany.

Chorus

Hurrah, hurrah, for Berlin on the Spree!
Hurrah, hurrah, there's 'Sossiges' for tea!
We're out to catch the Kaiser and to bring him to his knee,
While we go marching to Germany.

Jessie Pope

35

War Girls

There's the girl who clips your ticket for the train,
  And the girl who speeds the lift from floor to floor,
There's the girl who does a milk-round in the rain,
  And the girl who calls for orders at your door.
    Strong, sensible, and fit,
    They're out to show their grit,
  And tackle jobs with energy and knack.
    No longer caged and penned up,
    They're going to keep their end up
  Till the khaki soldier boys come marching back.

There's the motor girl who drives a heavy van,
  There's the butcher girl who brings your joint of meat,
There's the girl who cries 'All fares, please!' like a man,
  And the girl who whistles taxis up the street.
    Beneath each uniform
    Beats a heart that's soft and warm,
  Though of canny mother-wit they show no lack;
    But a solemn statement this is,
      They've no time for love and kisses
      Till the khaki soldier-boys come marching back.

Jessie Pope

The Call

Who's for the trench –
  Are you, my laddie?
Who'll follow French –
Will you, my laddie?
Who's fretting to begin,
Who's going out to win?
And who wants to save his skin –
Do you, my laddie?

Who's for the khaki suit –
Are you, my laddie?
Who longs to charge and shoot –
Do you, my laddie?
Who's keen on getting fit,
Who means to show his grit,
And who'd rather wait a bit –
Would you, my laddie?

Who'll earn the Empire's thanks –
Will you, my laddie?
Who'll swell the victor's ranks –
Will you, my laddie?
When that procession comes,
Banners and rolling drums –
Who'll stand and bite his thumbs –
Will you, my laddie?

Jessie Pope

Channel Firing

That night your great guns, unawares,
   Shook all our coffins as we lay,
And broke the chancel window-squares,
We thought it was the Judgment-day

And sat upright. While drearisome
Arose the howl of wakened hounds:
The mouse let fall the altar-crumb,
The worms drew back into the mounds,

The glebe cow drooled. Till God called, 'No;
It's gunnery practice out at sea
Just as before you went below;
The world is as it used to be:

'All nations striving strong to make
Red war yet redder. Mad as hatters
They do no more for Christés sake
Than you who are helpless in such matters.

'That this is not the judgment-hour
For some of them's a blessed thing,
For if it were they'd have to scour
Hell's floor for so much threatening...

'Ha, ha. It will be warmer when
I blow the trumpet (if indeed
I ever do; for you are men,
And rest eternal sorely need).'

So down we lay again. 'I wonder,
Will the world ever saner be',
Said one, 'than when He sent us under
In our indifferent century!'

And many a skeleton shook his head.
'Instead of preaching forty year',
My neighbour Parson Thirdly said,
'I wish I had stuck to pipes and beer.'

Again the guns disturbed the hour,
Roaring their readiness to avenge,
As far inland as Stourton Tower,
And Camelot, and starlit Stonehenge.

Thomas Hardy

A Call to National Service

Up and be doing, all who have a hand
To lift, a back to bend. It must not be
In times like these that vaguely linger we
To air our vaunts and hopes; and leave our land

Untended as a wild of weeds and sand.
– Say, then, 'I come!' and go, O women and men
Of palace, ploughshare, easel, counter, pen;
That scareless, scathless, England still may stand.

Would years but let me stir as once I stirred
At many a dawn to take the forward track,
And with a stride plunged on to enterprize,

I now would speed like yester wind that whirred
Through yielding pines; and serve with never a slack,
So loud for promptness all around outcries!

Thomas Hardy

40

The Man He Killed

'Had he and I but met
    By some old ancient inn,
We should have sat us down to wet
    Right many a nipperkin!

    'But ranged as infantry,
    And staring face to face,
I shot at him as he at me,
    And killed him in his place.

    'I shot him dead because –
    Because he was my foe,
Just so: my foe of course he was;
    That's clear enough; although

    'He thought he'd 'list, perhaps,
    Off-hand like – just as I –
Was out of work – had sold his traps –
    No other reason why.

    'Yes; quaint and curious war is!
    You shoot a fellow down
You'd treat if met where any bar is,
    Or help to half-a-crown.'

Thomas Hardy

Then and Now

When battles were fought
    With a chivalrous sense of should and ought,
  In spirit men said,
  'End we quick or dead,
  Honour is some reward!
Let us fight fair – for our own best or worst;
  So, Gentlemen of the Guard,
  Fire first!'

  In the open they stood,
Man to man in his knightlihood:
  They would not deign
  To profit by a stain
  On the honourable rules,
Knowing that practise perfidy no man durst
  Who in the heroic schools
  Was nurst.

  But now, behold, what
Is war with those where honour is not!
  Rama laments
  Its dead innocents;
  Herod howls: 'Sly slaughter
Rules now! Let us, by modes once called accurst,
  Overhead, under water,
  Stab first.'

Thomas Hardy

42

A War Poem

Lord, in this quarter of a hundred years,
What mighty progress in Thy world appears!
Though strife and loud dissensions do not cease,
Yet louder still is this great talk of Peace.

Red war exists, but stands in ill repute
Were Homer back among us with his lute
He could not, and he would not, sing of war;
For Peace is what the world is craving for.

Spurning old narrow paths, men's feet have trod
In larger ways, and found the larger God.
Now thy great truth is dimly understood –
Religion lies in loving brotherhood.

Ella Wheeler Wilcox

Woman and War

We women teach our little sons how wrong
    And how ignoble blows are; school and church
Support our precepts and inoculate
The growing minds with thoughts of love and peace.
'Let dogs delight to bark and bite', we say;
But human beings with immortal souls
Must rise above the methods of the brute,
And walk with reason and with self-control.

And then – dear God! you men, you wise, strong men,
Our self-announced superiors in brain,
Our peers in judgement, you go forth to war!
You leap at one another, mutilate
And starve and kill your fellow-men, and ask
The world's applause for such heroic deeds.
You boast and strut; and if no song is sung,
No laudatory epic writ in blood,
Telling how many widows you have made,
Why then, perforce, you say our bards are dead
And inspiration sleeps to wake no more.
And we, the women, we whose lives you are –

What can we do but sit in silent homes,
And wait and suffer? Not for us the blare
Of trumpets and the bugle's call to arms –
For us no waving banners, no supreme
Triumphant hour of conquest. Ours the slow
Dread torture of uncertainty, each day
The bootless battle with the same despair,

And when at best your victories reach our ears,
There reaches with them, to our pitying hearts,
The thought of countless homes made desolate,
And other women weeping for their dead.

O men, wise men, superior beings, say,
Is there no substitute for war in this
Great age and era? If you answer 'No',
Then let us rear our children to be wolves,
And teach them from the cradle how to kill.
Why should we women waste our time and words
In talking peace, when men declare for war?

Ella Wheeler Wilcox

My Boy Jack

'Have you news of my boy Jack?'
    Not this tide.
'When d'you think that he'll come back?'
Not with this wind blowing, and this tide.

'Has any one else had word of him?'
Not this tide.
For what is sunk will hardly swim,
Not with this wind blowing, and this tide.

'Oh, dear, what comfort can I find?'
None this tide,
Nor any tide,
Except he did not shame his kind —
Not even with that wind blowing, and that tide.

Then hold your head up all the more,
This tide,
And every tide;
Because he was the son you bore,
And gave to that wind blowing and that tide.

Rudyard Kipling

Gethsemane

The Garden called Gethsemane
  In Picardy it was,
And there the people came to see
  The English soldiers pass.
We used to pass – we used to pass
  Or halt, as it might be,
And ship our masks in case of gas
  Beyond Gethsemane.

The Garden called Gethsemane,
  It held a pretty lass,
But all the time she talked to me
  I prayed my cup might pass.
The officer sat on the chair,
  The men lay on the grass,
And all the time we halted there
  I prayed my cup might pass –

It didn't pass – it didn't pass –
  It didn't pass from me.
I drank it when we met the gas
  Beyond Gethsemane.

Rudyard Kipling

For All We Have and Are

For all we have and are,
    For all our children's fate,
Stand up and take the war.
The Hun is at the gate!
Our world has passed away,
In wantonness o'erthrown.
There is nothing left to-day
But steel and fire and stone!

Though all we knew depart,
The old Commandments stand: —
'In courage kept your heart,
In strength lift up your hand.'

Once more we hear the word
That sickened earth of old: —
'No law except the Sword

48

Unsheathed and uncontrolled.'
Once more it knits mankind,
Once more the nations go
To meet and break and bind
A crazed and driven foe.

Comfort, content, delight,
The ages' slow-bought gain,
They shrivelled in a night.
Only ourselves remain
To face the naked days
In silent fortitude,
Through perils and dismays
Renewed and re-renewed.

Though all we made depart,
The old Commandments stand: –
'In patience keep your heart,
In strength lift up your hand.'

No easy hope or lies
Shall bring us to our goal,
But iron sacrifice
Of body, will, and soul.
There is but one task for all –
One life for each to give.
What stands if Freedom fall?
Who dies if England live?

Rudyard Kipling

Attack

At dawn the ridge emerges massed and dun
In the wild purple of the glow'ring sun,
Smouldering through spouts of drifting smoke that shroud
The menacing scarred slope; and, one by one,
Tanks creep and topple forward to the wire.
The barrage roars and lifts. Then, clumsily bowed
With bombs and guns and shovels and battle-gear,
Men jostle and climb to, meet the bristling fire.
Lines of grey, muttering faces, masked with fear,
They leave their trenches, going over the top,
While time ticks blank and busy on their wrists,
And hope, with furtive eyes and grappling fists,
Flounders in mud. O Jesus, make it stop!

Siegfried Sassoon

Does it Matter?

Does it matter? – losing your legs?...
For people will always be kind,
And you need not show that you mind
When others come in after hunting
To gobble their muffins and eggs.

Does it matter? – losing your sight?...
There's such splendid work for the blind;
And people will always be kind,
As you sit on the terrace remembering
And turning your face to the light.

Do they matter? – those dreams in the pit?...
You can drink and forget and be glad,
And people won't say that you're mad;
For they know that you've fought for your country
And no one will worry a bit.

Siegfried Sassoon

Suicide in the Trenches

I knew a simple soldier boy
Who grinned at life in empty joy,
Slept soundly through the lonesome dark,
And whistled early with the lark.

In winter trenches, cowed and glum,
With crumps and lice and lack of rum,
He put a bullet through his brain.
No one spoke of him again.

You smug-faced crowds with kindling eye
Who cheer when soldier lads march by,
Sneak home and pray you'll never know
The hell where youth and laughter go.

Siegfried Sassoon

Reconciliation

When you are standing at your hero's grave,
  Or near some homeless village where he died,
Remember, through your heart's rekindling pride,
The German soldiers who were loyal and brave.

Men fought like brutes; and hideous things were done;
And you have nourished hatred,, harsh and blind.
But in that Golgotha perhaps you'll find
The mothers of the men who killed your son.

Siegfried Sassoon

To Germany

You are blind like us. Your hurt no man designed,
  And no man claimed the conquest of your land.
But gropers both, through fields of thought confined,
We stumble and we do not understand.
You only saw your future bigly planned,
And we the tapering paths of our own mind,
And in each other's dearest ways we stand,
And hiss and hate. And the blind fight the blind.

When it is peace, then we may view again
With new-won eyes each other's truer form,
And wonder. Grown more loving-kind and warm
We'll grasp firm hands and laugh at the old pain,
When it is peace. But until peace, the storm,
The darkness and the thunder and the rain.

Charles Hamilton Sorley

When You See Millions of the Mouthless Dead

When you see millions of the mouthless dead
    Across your dreams in pale battalions go,
Say not soft things as other men have said,
That you'll remember. For you need not so.
Give them not praise. For, deaf, how should they know
It is not curses heaped on each gashed head?
Nor tears. Their blind eyes see not your tears flow.
Nor honour. It is easy to be dead.
Say only this, 'They are dead'. Then add thereto,
'Yet many a better one has died before.'
Then, scanning all the o'ercrowded mass, should you
Perceive one face that you loved heretofore,
It is a spook. None wears the face you knew.
Great death has made all his for evermore.

Charles Hamilton Sorley

All the Hills and Vales Along

All the hills and vales along
Earth is bursting into song,
And the singers are the chaps
Who are going to die perhaps.
O sing, marching men,
Till the valleys ring again.
Give your gladness to earth's keeping,
So be glad, when you are sleeping.

Cast away regret and rue,
Think what you are marching to.
Little live, great pass.
Jesus Christ and Barabbas
Were found the same day.
This died, that went his way.
So sing with joyful breath,
For why, you are going to death.
Teeming earth will surely store
All the gladness that you pour.

Earth that never doubts nor fears,
Earth that knows of death, not tears,
Earth that bore with joyful ease
Hemlock for Socrates,
Earth that blossomed and was glad
'Neath the cross that Christ had,
Shall rejoice and blossom too
When the bullet reaches you.
Wherefore, men marching
On the road to death, sing!
Pour your gladness on earth's head,
So be merry, so be dead.

From the hills and valleys earth
Shouts back the sound of mirth,
Tramp of feet and lilt of song
Ringing all the road along.
All the music of their going,
Ringing swinging glad song-throwing,
Earth will echo still, when foot
Lies numb and voice mute.
On, marching men, on
To the gates of death with song.
Sow your gladness for earth's reaping,
So you may be glad, though sleeping.
Strew your gladness on earth's bed,
So be merry, so be dead.

Charles Hamilton Sorley

Pro Patria

England, in this great fight to which you go
    Because, where Honour calls you, go you must,
Be glad, whatever comes, at least to know
      You have your quarrel just.

Peace was your care; before the nations' bar
  Her cause you pleaded and her ends you sought;
But not for her sake, being what you are,
      Could you be bribed and bought.

Others may spurn the pledge of land to land,
  May with the brute sword stain a gallant past;
But by the seal to which you set your hand,
      Thank God, you still stand fast!

Forth, then, to front that peril of the deep
  With smiling lips and in your eyes the light,
Steadfast and confident, of those who keep
      Their storied 'scutcheon bright.

And we, whose burden is to watch and wait –
  High-hearted ever, strong in faith and prayer,
We ask what offering we may consecrate,
      What humble service share.

To steel our souls against the lust of ease;
 To find out welfare in the common good;
To hold together, marging all degrees
     In one wide brotherhood; –

To teach that he who saves himself is lost;
To bear in silence though our hearts my bleed;
To spend ourselves, and never count the cost,
For others' greater need; –

To go our quiet ways, subdued and sane;
 To hush all vulgar clamour of the street;
With level calm to face alike the strain
     Of triumph or defeat; –

This be our part, for so we serve you best,
 So best confirm their prowess and their pride,
Your warrior sons, to whom in this high test
     Our fortunes we confide.

Owen Seaman

To Belgium in Exile

L and of the desolate, Mother of tears,
Weeping your beauty marred and torn,
Your children tossed upon the spears,
Your altars rent, your hearths forlorn,
Where Spring has no renewing spell,
And Love no language save a long Farewell!

Ah, precious tears, and each a pearl,
Whose price-for so in God we trust
Who saw them fall in that blind swirl
Of ravening flame and reeking dust –
The spoiler with his life shall pay,
When Justice at the last demands her Day.

O tried and proved, whose record stands
Lettered in blood too deep to fade,
Take courage! Never in our hands
Shall the avenging sword be stayed
Till you are healed of all your pain,
And come with Honour to your own again.

Owen Seaman

Release

There is a healing magic in the night,
  The breeze blows cleaner than it did by day,
Forgot the fever of the fuller light,
And sorrow sinks insensibly away
As if some saint a cool white hand did lay
Upon the brow, and calm the restless brain.
The moon looks down with pale unpassioned ray –
Sufficient for the hour is its pain.
Be still and feel the night that hides away earth's stain.

Be still and loose the sense of God in you,
Be still and send your soul into the all,
The vasty distance where the stars shine blue,
No longer antlike on the earth to crawl.
Released from time and sense of great or small,
Float on the pinions of the Night-Queen's wings;
Soar till the swift inevitable fall
Will drag you back into all the world's small things;
Yet for an hour be one with all escaped things.

Colwyn Phylipps

Keep the Home Fires Burning

They were summoned from the hill-side,
   They were called in from the glen,
And the Country found them ready
At the stirring call for men.

Let no tears add to their hardship;
As the Soldiers pass along
And although your heart is breaking,
Make it sing this cheery song.

Chorus:

Keep the Home-fires burning,
While your hearts are yearning,
Though your lads are far away
They dream of Home;
There's a silver lining
   Through the dark cloud shining,
      Turn the dark cloud inside out,
         Till the boys come Home.

Verse:

Over seas there came a pleading
'Help a Nation in distress,'
And we gave our glorious laddies;
Honor made us do no less.

For no gallant Son of Freedom
To a tyrant's yoke should bend,
And a noble heart must answer
To the sacred call of 'Friend'.

Chorus:

Keep the Home-fires burning,
While your hearts are yearning,
Though your lads are far away
They dream of Home;
There's a silver lining
Through the dark cloud shining,
Turn the dark cloud inside out,
Till the boys come Home.

Lena Gilbert Ford

Marching Men

Under the level winter sky
I saw a thousand Christs go by.
They sang an idle song and free
As they went up to calvary.

Careless of eye and coarse of lip,
They marched in holiest fellowship.
That heaven might heal the world, they gave
Their earth-born dreams to deck the grave.

With souls unpurged and steadfast breath
They supped the sacrament of death.
And for each one, far off, apart,
Seven swords have rent a woman's heart.

Marjorie Pickthall

Canada to England

Great names of thy great captains gone before
Beat with our blood, who have that blood of thee:
Raleigh and Grenville, Wolfe, and all the free
Fine souls who dared to front a world in war.
Such only may outreach the envious years
Where feebler crowns and fainter stars remove,
Nurtured in one remembrance and one love
Too high for passion and too stern for tears.

O little isle our fathers held for home,
Not, not alone thy standards and thy hosts
Lead where thy sons shall follow, Mother Land:
Quick as the north wind, ardent as the foam,
Behold, behold the invulnerable ghosts
Of all past greatnesses about thee stand.

Marjorie Pickthall

Belgium

La Belgique ne regrette rien

ot with her ruined silver spires,
   Not with her cities shamed and rent,
Perish the imperishable fires
That shape the homestead from the tent.

Wherever men are staunch and free,
There shall she keep her fearless state,
And homeless, to great nations be
The home of all that makes them great.

Edith Wharton

Joining the Colours

There they go marching all in step so gay!
  Smooth-cheeked and golden, food for shells and guns.
Blithely they go as to a wedding day,
The mothers' sons.

The drab street stares to see them row on row
On the high tram-tops, singing like the lark.
Too careless-gay for courage, singing they go
Into the dark.

With tin whistles, mouth-organs, any noise,
They pipe the way to glory and the grave;
Foolish and young, the gay and golden boys
Love cannot save.

High heart! High courage! The poor girls they kissed
Run with them: they shall kiss no more, alas!
Out of the mist they stepped-into the mist
Singing they pass.

Katharine Tynan

The Broken Soldier

The broken soldier sings and whistles day to dark;
   He's but the remnant of a man, maimed and half-blind,
But the soul they could not harm goes singing like the lark,
   Like the incarnate Joy that will not be confined.

The Lady at the Hall has given him a light task,
   He works in the gardens as busy as a bee;
One hand is but a stump and his face a pitted mask;
   The gay soul goes singing like a bird set free.

Whistling and singing like a linnet on wings;
   The others stop to listen, leaning on the spade,
Whole men and comely, they fret at little things.
   The soul of him's singing like a thrush in a glade.

Hither and thither, hopping, like Robin on the grass,
   The soul in the broken man is beautiful and brave;
And while he weeds the pansies and the bright hours pass
   The bird caught in the cage whistles its joyous stave.

Katharine Tynan

Trenches, St Eloi

Over the flat slopes of St Eloi
    A wide wall of sand bags.
Night,
In the silence desultory men
Pottering over small fires, cleaning their mess-tins:
To and fro, from the lines,
Men walk as on Piccadilly,
Making paths in the dark,
Through scattered dead horses,
Over a dead Belgian's belly.

The Germans have rockets. The English have no rockets.
Behind the line, cannon, hidden, lying back miles.
Behind the line, chaos:

My mind is a corridor. The minds about me are corridors.
Nothing suggests itself. There is nothing to do but keep on.

T. E. Hulme

Rouge Bouquet

In a wood they call the Rouge Bouquet
There is a new-made grave to-day,
Built by never a spade nor pick
Yet covered with earth ten metres thick.
There lie many fighting men,
Dead in their youthful prime,
Never to laugh nor love again
Nor taste the Summertime.
For Death came flying through the air
And stopped his flight at the dugout stair,
Touched his prey and left them there,
Clay to clay.
He hid their bodies stealthily
In the soil of the land they fought to free
And fled away.
Now over the grave abrupt and clear
Three volleys ring;
And perhaps their brave young spirits hear
The bugle sing:
'Go to sleep!
Go to sleep!
Slumber well where the shell screamed and fell.
Let your rifles rest on the muddy floor,
You will not need them any more.
Danger's past;
Now at last,
Go to sleep!'

There is on earth no worthier grave
To hold the bodies of the brave
Than this place of pain and pride
Where they nobly fought and nobly died.
Never fear but in the skies
Saints and angels stand
Smiling with their holy eyes
On this new-come band.
St. Michael's sword darts through the air
And touches the aureole on his hair
As he sees them stand saluting there,
His stalwart sons;
And Patrick, Brigid, Columkill
Rejoice that in veins of warriors still
The Gael's blood runs.
And up to Heaven's doorway floats,
From the wood called Rouge Bouquet
A delicate cloud of bugle notes
That softly say:
'Farewell!
Farewell!
Comrades true, born anew, peace to you!
Your souls shall be where the heroes are
And your memory shine like the morning-star.
Brave and dear,
Shield us here.
Farewell!'

Joyce Kilmer

Trojan War

We care not what old Homer tells
    Of Trojan War and Helen's fame;
Upon the ancient Dardanelles
New peoples write – in blood – their name.

Those Grecian heroes long have fled;
No more the Plain of Troy they haunt:
Made sacred by our Southern dead,
Historic is the Hellespont.

Homeric wars are fought again
By men who like old Greeks can die;
Australian back-block heroes slain
With Hector and Achilles lie.

No legend lured these men to roam;
They journeyed forth to save from harm
Some Mother – Helen sad at home,
Some obscure Helen on a farm.

And, when one falls upon the hill,
Then, by dark Styx's gloomy strand,
In honour to plain Private Bill
Great Agamemnon lifts his hand!

Arthur Henry Adams

To My Daughter Betty, The Gift of God

In wiser days, my darling rosebud, blown
To beauty proud as was your mother's prime,
In that desired, delayed, incredible time,
You'll ask why I abandoned you, my own,
And the dear heart that was your baby throne,
To dice with death. And oh! they'll give you rhyme
And reason: some will call the thing sublime,
And some decry it in a knowing tone.
So here, while the mad guns curse overhead,
And tired men sigh with mud for couch and floor,
Know that we fools, now with the foolish dead,
Died not for flag, nor King, nor Emperor, –
But for a dream, born in a herdsman's shed,
And for the secret Scripture of the poor.

T. M. Kettle

Field Ambulance in Retreat

Via Dolorosa, Via Sacra

I

A straight flagged road, laid on the rough earth,
A causeway of stone from beautiful city to city,
Between the tall trees, the slender, delicate trees,
Through the flat green land, by plots of flowers, by black
  canals thick with heat.

II

The road-makers made it well
Of fine stone, strong for the feet of the oxen and of the great
  Flemish horses,
And for the high waggons piled with corn from the harvest.
But the labourers are few;
They and their quiet oxen stand aside and wait
By the long road loud with the passing of the guns, the rush
  of armoured cars and the tramp of an army on the
  march forward to battle;
And, where the piled corn-waggons went, our dripping
  Ambulance carries home
Its red and white harvest from the fields.

III

The straight flagged road breaks into dust, into a thin
    white cloud,
About the feet of a regiment driven back league by league,
Rifles at trail, and standards wrapped in black funeral cloths.
    Unhasting, proud in retreat,
They smile as the Red Cross Ambulance rushes by.
(You know nothing of beauty and of desolation who
    have not seen
That smile of an army in retreat.)
They go: and our shining, beckoning danger goes
    with them,
And our joy in the harvests that we gathered in at
    nightfall in the fields;
And like an unloved hand laid on a beating heart
Our safety weighs us down.
Safety hard and strange; stranger and yet more hard
As, league after dying league, the beautiful, desolate Land,
Falls back from the intolerable speed of an Ambulance in
    retreat
On the sacred, dolorous Way.

May Sinclair

The Day's March

The battery grides and jingles,
  Mile succeeds to mile;
Shaking the noonday sunshine
The guns lunge out awhile,
And then are still awhile.

We amble along the highway;
The reeking, powdery dust
Ascends and cakes our faces
With a striped, sweaty crust.

Under the still sky's violet
The heat throbs on the air...
The white road's dusty radiance
Assumes a dark glare.

With a head hot and heavy,
And eyes that cannot rest,
And a black heart burning
In a stifled breast,

I sit in the saddle,
I feel the road unroll,
And keep my senses straightened
Toward to-morrow's goal.

There, over unknown meadows
Which we must reach at last,
Day and night thunders
A black and chilly blast.

Heads forget heaviness,
Hearts forget spleen,
For by that mighty winnowing
Being is blown clean.

Light in the eyes again,
Strength in the hand,
A spirit dares, dies, forgives,
And can understand!

And, best! Love comes back again
After grief and shame,
And along the wind of death
Throws a clean flame.

The battery grides and jingles,
Mile succeeds to mile;
Suddenly battering the silence
The guns burst out awhile...

I lift my head and smile.

Robert Nichols

Noon

It is midday; the deep trench glares.....
A buzz and blaze of flies....
The hot wind puffs the giddy airs....
The great sun rakes the skies.

No sound in all the stagnant trench
Where forty standing men
Endure the sweat and grit and stench,
Like cattle in a pen.

Sometimes a sniper's bullet whirs
Or twangs the whining wire,
Sometimes a soldier sighs and stirs
As in hell's frying fire.

From out a high, cool cloud descends
An aeroplane's far moan,
The sun strikes down, the thin cloud rends....
The black speck travels on.

And sweating, dazed, isolate
In the hot trench beneath,
We bide the next shrewd move of fate
Be it of life or death.

Robert Nichols

Dreams in War Time

I

I wandered through a house of many rooms.
It grew darker and darker,
Until, at last, I could only find my way
By passing my fingers along the wall.
Suddenly my hand shot through an open window,
And the thorn of a rose I could not see
Pricked it so sharply
That I cried aloud.

II

I dug a grave under an oak-tree.
With infinite care, I stamped my spade
Into the heavy grass.
The sod sucked it,
And I drew it out with effort,
Watching the steel run liquid in the moonlight
As it came clear.
I stooped, and dug, and never turned,
For behind me,
On the dried leaves,
My own face lay like a white pebble,
Waiting.

III

I gambled with a silver money.
The dried seed-vessels of 'honesty'
Were stacked in front of me.
Dry, white years slipping through my fingers
One by one.
One by one, gathered by the Croupier.

'Faites vos jeux, Messieurs.'
I staked on the red,
And the black won.
Dry years,
Dead years;
But I had a system,
I always staked on the red.

IV

I painted the leaves of bushes red
And shouted: 'Fire! Fire!'
But the neighbors only laughed.
'We cannot warm our hands at them', they said.
Then they cut down my bushes,
And made a bonfire,
And danced about it.
But I covered my face and wept,
For ashes are not beautiful
Even in the dawn.

V

I followed a procession of singing girls
Who danced to the glitter of tambourines.
Where the street turned at a lighted corner,
I caught the purple dress of one of the dancers,
But, as I grasped it, it tore,
And the purple dye ran from it
Like blood
Upon the ground.

VI

I wished to post a letter,
  But although I paid much,
    Still the letter was overweight.
    'What is in this package?' said the clerk,
    'It is very heavy.'
    'Yes', I said,
    'And yet it is only a dried fruit.'

VII

I had made a kite,
On it I had pasted golden stars
And white torches,
And the tail was spotted scarlet like a tiger-lily,
    And very long.
        I flew my kite,
          And my soul was contented
            Watching it flash against the concave of the sky.
            My friends pointed at the clouds;
            They begged me to take in my kite.
          But I was happy
        Seeing the mirror shock of it
    Against the black clouds.
Then the lightning came
And struck the kite.
It puffed – blazed – fell.
But still I walked on,
In the drowning rain,
Slowly winding up the string.

Amy Lowell

September, 1918

This afternoon was the colour of
   water falling through sunlight;
The trees glittered with the tumbling of leaves;
The sidewalks shone like alleys of dropped maple leaves,
And the houses ran along them laughing out of square,
   open windows.
Under a tree in the park,
Two little boys, lying flat on their faces,
Were carefully gathering red berries
To put in a pasteboard box.
Some day there will be no war,
Then I shall take out this afternoon
And turn it in my fingers,
And remark the sweet taste of it upon my palate,
And note the crisp variety of its flights of leaves.
To-day I can only gather it
And put it into my lunch-box,
For I have time for nothing
But the endeavour to balance myself
Upon a broken world.

Amy Lowell

The Target

I shot him, and it had to be
One of us 'Twas him or me.
'Couldn't be helped' and none can blame
Me, for you would do the same

My mother, she can't sleep for fear
Of what might be a-happening here
To me. Perhaps it might be best
To die, and set her fears at rest

For worst is worst, and worry's done.
Perhaps he was the only son. . .
Yet God keeps still, and does not say
A word of guidance anyway.

Well, if they get me, first I'll find
That boy, and tell him all my mind,
And see who felt the bullet worst,
And ask his pardon, if I durst.

All's a tangle. Here's my job.
A man might rave, or shout, or sob;
And God He takes takes no sort of heed.
This is a bloody mess indeed.

Ivor Gurney

To His Love

He's gone, and all our plans
  Are useless indeed.
We'll walk no more on Cotswold
  Where the sheep feed
  Quietly and take no heed.

His body that was so quick
  Is not as you
Knew it, on Severn river
  Under the blue
  Driving our small boat through.

You would not know him now ...
  But still he died
Nobly, so cover him over
  With violets of pride
  Purple from Severn side.

Cover him, cover him soon!
  And with thick-set
Masses of memoried flowers –
  Hide that red wet
  Thing I must somehow forget.

Ivor Gurney

84

In No Man's Land

The hedge on the left, and the trench on the right,
  And the whispering, rustling wood between,
And who knows where in the wood to-night
Death or capture may lurk unseen.
The open field and the figures lying
Under the shade of the apple trees –
Is it the wind in the branches sighing
Or a German trying to stop a sneeze?

Louder the voices of night come thronging,
But over them all the sound is clear,
Taking me back to the place of my longing
And the cultured sneezes I used to hear.
Lecture-time and my tutor's 'hanker'
Stopping his period's rounded close,
Like the frozen hand of a German ranker
Down in a ditch with a cold in his nose.

I'm cold, too, and a stealthy shuffle
From the man with a pistol covering me,
And the Bosche moving off with a snap and a shuffle
Break the windows of memory –
I can't make sure till the moon gets lighter –
Anyway shooting is over bold.
Oh, damn you, get back to your trench, you blighter,
I really can't shoot a man with a cold.

E. Alan Mackintosh

Ghosts of War

When you and I are buried
    With grasses over head,
The memory of our fights will stand
Above this bare and tortured land,
We knew ere we were dead.

Though grasses grow at Vimy,
And poppies at Messines,
And in High Wood the children play,
The craters and the graves will stay
To show what things have been.

Though all be quiet in day-time,
The night shall bring a change,
And peasants walking home will see
Shell-torn meadow and riven tree,
And their own fields grown strange.

They shall hear live men crying,
They shall see dead men lie,
Shall hear the rattling Maxims fire,
And by the broken twists of wire
Gold flares light up the sky.

And in their new-built houses
The frightened folk will see
Pale bombers coming down the street,
And hear the flurry of charging feet,
And the crash of Victory.

This is our Earth baptizèd
With the red wine of War.
Horror and courage hand in hand
Shall brood upon the stricken land
In silence evermore.

E. Alan Mackintosh

Clifton Chapel

This is the Chapel: here, my son,
   Your father thought the thoughts of youth,
And heard the words that one by one
The touch of Life has turn'd to truth.
Here in a day that is not far,
You too may speak with noble ghosts
Of manhood and the vows of war
You made before the Lord of Hosts.

To set the cause above renown,
To love the game beyond the prize,
To honour, while you strike him down,
The foe that comes with fearless eyes;
To count the life of battle good,
And dear the land that gave you birth,
And dearer yet the brotherhood
That binds the brave of all the earth. —

My son, the oath is yours: the end
Is His, Who built the world of strife,
Who gave His children Pain for friend,
And Death for surest hope of life.
To-day and here the fight's begun,
Of the great fellowship you're free;
Henceforth the School and you are one,
And what You are, the race shall be.

God send you fortune: yet be sure,
Among the lights that gleam and pass,
You'll live to follow none more pure
Than that which glows on yonder brass:
'Qui procul hinc,' the legend's writ, —
The frontier-grave is far away —
'Qui ante diem periit:
Sed miles, sed pro patria.'

Sir Henry Newbolt

Vitaï Lampada

There's a breathless hush in the Close to-night –
　　Ten to make and the match to win –
A bumping pitch and a blinding light,
An hour to play and the last man in.
And it's not for the sake of a ribboned coat,
Or the selfish hope of a season's fame,
But his captain's hand on his shoulder smote
'Play up! play up! and play the game! '

The sand of the desert is sodden red, –
Red with the wreck of a square that broke; –
The Gatling's jammed and the Colonel dead,
And the regiment blind with dust and smoke.
The river of death has brimmed his banks,
And England's far, and Honour a name,
But the voice of a schoolboy rallies the ranks:
'Play up! play up! and play the game! '

This is the word that year by year,
While in her place the school is set,
Every one of her sons must hear,
And none that hears it dare forget.
This they all with a joyful mind
Bear through life like a torch in flame,
And falling fling to the host behind –
'Play up! play up! and play the game!

Sir Henry Newbolt

The Aisne, 1914–15

We first saw fire on the tragic slopes
      Where the flood-tide of France's early gain,
Big with wrecked promise and abandoned hopes,
Broke in a surf of blood along the Aisne.

The charge her heroes left us, we assumed,
What, dying, they reconquered, we preserved,
In the chill trenches, harried, shelled, entombed,
Winter came down on us, but no man swerved.

Winter came down on us. The low clouds, torn
In the stark branches of the riven pines,
Blurred the white rockets that from dusk till morn
Traced the wide curve of the close-grappling lines.

In rain, and fog that on the withered hill
Froze before dawn, the lurking foe drew down;
Or light snows fell that made forlorner still
The ravaged country and the ruined town;

Or the long clouds would end. Intensely fair,
The winter constellations blazing forth –
Perseus, the Twins, Orion, the Great Bear –
Gleamed on our bayonets pointing to the north.

And the lone sentinel would start and soar
On wings of strong emotion as he knew
That kinship with the stars that only War
Is great enough to lift man's spirit to.

And ever down the curving front, aglow
With the pale rockets' intermittent light,
He heard, like distant thunder, growl and grow
The rumble of far battles in the night, –

Rumors, reverberant indistinct, remote,
Borne from red fields whose martial names have won
The power to thrill like a far trumpet-note, –
Vic, Vailly, Soupir, Hurtelise, Craonne . . .

Craonne, before thy cannon-swept plateau,
Where like sere leaves lay strewn September's dead,
I found for all dear things I forfeited
A recompense I would not now forego.

For that high fellowship was ours then
With those who, championing another's good,
More than dull Peace or its poor votaries could,
Taught us the dignity of being men.

There we drained deeper the deep cup of life,
And on sublimer summits came to learn,
After soft things, the terrible and stern,
After sweet Love, the majesty of Strife;

There where we faced under those frowning heights
The blast that maims, the hurricane that kills;
There where the watchlights on the winter hills
Flickered like balefire through inclement nights;

There where, firm links in the unyielding chain,
Where fell the long-planned blow and fell in vain –
Hearts worthy of the honor and the trial,
We helped to hold the lines along the Aisne.

Alan Seeger

Champagne, 1914–15

In the glad revels, in the happy fêtes,
When cheeks are flushed, and glasses gilt and pearled
With the sweet wine of France that concentrates
The sunshine and the beauty of the world,

Drink sometimes, you whose footsteps yet may tread
The undisturbed, delightful paths of Earth,
To those whose blood, in pious duty shed,
Hallows the soil where that same wine had birth.

Here, by devoted comrades laid away,
Along our lines they slumber where they fell,
Beside the crater at the Ferme d'Alger
And up the bloody slopes of La Pompelle,

And round the city whose cathedral towers
The enemies of Beauty dared profane,
And in the mat of multicolored flowers
That clothe the sunny chalk-fields of Champagne.

Under the little crosses where they rise
The soldier rests. Now round him undismayed
The cannon thunders, and at night he lies
At peace beneath the eternal fusillade. ...

That other generations might possess –
From shame and menace free in years to come –
A richer heritage of happiness,
He marched to that heroic martyrdom.

Esteeming less the forfeit that he paid
Than undishonored that his flag might float

Over the towers of liberty, he made
His breast the bulwark and his blood the moat.

Obscurely sacrificed, his nameless tomb,
Bare of the sculptor's art, the poet's lines,
Summer shall flush with poppy-fields in bloom,
And Autumn yellow with maturing vines.

There the grape-pickers at their harvesting
Shall lightly tread and load their wicker trays,
Blessing his memory as they toil and sing
In the slant sunshine of October days. ...

I love to think that if my blood should be
So privileged to sink where his has sunk,
I shall not pass from Earth entirely,
But when the banquet rings, when healths are drunk,

And faces that the joys of living fill
Glow radiant with laughter and good cheer,
In beaming cups some spark of me shall still
Brim toward the lips that once I held so dear.

So shall one coveting no higher plane
Than nature clothes in color and flesh and tone,
Even from the grave put upward to attain
The dreams youth cherished and missed and might
   have known;

And that strong need that strove unsatisfied
Toward earthly beauty in all forms it wore,
Not death itself shall utterly divide,
From the belovèd shapes it thirsted for.

Alas, how many an adept for whose arms
Life held delicious offerings perished here,
How many in the prime of all that charms,
Crowned with all gifts that conquer and endear!

Honor them not so much with tears and flowers,
But you with whom the sweet fulfilment lies,
Where in the anguish of atrocious hours
Turned their last thoughts and closed their dying eyes,

Rather when music on bright gatherings lays
Its tender spell, and joy is uppermost,
Be mindful of the men they were, and raise
Your glasses to them in one silent toast.

Drink to them – amorous of dear Earth as well,
They asked no tribute lovelier than this –
And in the wine that ripened where they fell,
Oh, frame your lips as though it were a kiss.

Alan Seeger

I Have a Rendezvous with Death

I have a rendezvous with Death
At some disputed barricade,
When Spring comes back with rustling shade
And apple-blossoms fill the air –
I have a rendezvous with Death
When Spring brings back blue days and fair.

It may be he shall take my hand
And lead me into his dark land
And close my eyes and quench my breath –
It may be I shall pass him still.
I have a rendezvous with Death
On some scarred slope of battered hill,
When Spring comes round again this year
And the first meadow-flowers appear.

God knows 'twere better to be deep
Pillowed in silk and scented down,
Where Love throbs out in blissful sleep,
Pulse nigh to pulse, and breath to breath,
Where hushed awakenings are dear ...
But I've a rendezvous with Death
At midnight in some flaming town,
When Spring trips north again this year,
And I to my pledged word am true,
I shall not fail that rendezvous.

Alan Seeger

In Memoriam (Easter, 1915)

The flowers left thick at nightfall in the wood
  This Eastertide call into mind the men,
Now far from home, who, with their sweethearts, should
Have gathered them and will do never again.

Edward Thomas

Rain

Rain, midnight rain, nothing but the wild rain
On this bleak hut, and solitude, and me
Remembering again that I shall die
And neither hear the rain nor give it thanks
For washing me cleaner than I have been
Since I was born into solitude.
Blessed are the dead that the rain rains upon:
But here I pray that none whom once I loved
Is dying tonight or lying still awake
Solitary, listening to the rain,
Either in pain or thus in sympathy
Helpless among the living and the dead,
Like a cold water among broken reeds,
Myriads of broken reeds all still and stiff,
Like me who have no love which this wild rain
Has not dissolved except the love of death,
If love it be towards what is perfect and
Cannot, the tempest tells me, disappoint.

Edward Thomas

Out in the Dark

Out in the dark over the snow
The fallow fawns invisible go
With the fallow doe;
And the winds blow
Fast as the stars are slow.

Stealthily the dark haunts round
And, when the lamp goes, without sound
At a swifter bound
Than the swiftest hound,
Arrives, and all else is drowned;

And star and I and wind and deer,
Are in the dark together, – near,
Yet far, – and fear
Drums on my ear
In that sage company drear.

How weak and little is the light,
All the universe of sight,
Love and delight,
Before the might,
If you love it not, of night.

Edward Thomas

Aldestrop

Yes. I remember Adlestrop —
  The name, because one afternoon
Of heat the express-train drew up there
Unwontedly. It was late June.

The steam hissed. Someone cleared his throat.
No one left and no one came
On the bare platform. What I saw
Was Adlestrop — only the name

And willows, willow-herb, and grass,
And meadowsweet, and haycocks dry,
No whit less still and lonely fair
Than the high cloudlets in the sky.

And for that minute a blackbird sang
Close by, and round him, mistier,
Farther and farther, all the birds
Of Oxfordshire and Gloucestershire.

Edward Thomas

Gone, Gone Again

Gone, gone again,
May, June, July,
And August gone,
Again gone by,

Not memorable
Save that I saw them go,
As past the empty quays
The rivers flow.

And now again,
In the harvest rain,
The Blenheim oranges
Fall grubby from the trees,

As when I was young –
And when the lost one was here –
And when the war began
To turn young men to dung.

Look at the old house,
Outmoded, dignified,
Dark and untenanted,
With grass growing instead

Of the footsteps of life,
The friendliness, the strife;
In its beds have lain
Youth, love, age, and pain:

I am something like that;
Only I am not dead,
Still breathing and interested
In the house that is not dark: —

I am something like that:
Not one pane to reflect the sun,
For the schoolboys to throw at —
They have broken every one.

Edward Thomas

Ypres

On the road to Ypres, on the long road,
   Marching strong,
We'll sing a song of Ypres, of her glory
And her wrong.

Proud rose her towers in the old time,
Long ago.
Trees stood on her ramparts, and the water
Lay below.

Shattered are the towers into potsherds –
Jumbled stones.
Underneath the ashes that were rafters
Whiten bones.

Blood is in the cellar where the wine was,
On the floor.
Rats run on the pavement where the wives met
At the door.

But in Ypres there's an army that is biding,
Seen of none.
You'd never hear their tramp nor see their shadow
In the sun.

Thousands of the dead men there are waiting
Through the night,
Waiting for a bugle in the cold dawn
Blown for fight.

Listen when the bugle's calling Forward!
They'll be found,
Dead men, risen in battalions
From underground,

Charging with us home, and through the foemen
Driving fear
Swifter than the madness in a madman,
As they hear

Dead men ring the bells of Ypres
For a sign,
Hear the bells and fear them in the Hunland
Over Rhine!

Laurence Binyon

For the Fallen

With proud thanksgiving, a mother for her children,
England mourns for her dead across the sea.
Flesh of her flesh they were, spirit of her spirit,
Fallen in the cause of the free.

Solemn the drums thrill; Death august and royal
Sings sorrow up into immortal spheres,
There is music in the midst of desolation
And a glory that shines upon our tears.

They went with songs to the battle, they were young,
Straight of limb, true of eye, steady and aglow.
They were staunch to the end against odds uncounted;
They fell with their faces to the foe.

They shall grow not old, as we that are left grow old:
Age shall not weary them, nor the years condemn.
At the going down of the sun and in the morning
We will remember them.

They mingle not with their laughing comrades again;
They sit no more at familiar tables of home;
They have no lot in our labour of the day-time;
They sleep beyond England's foam.

But where our desires are and our hopes profound,
Felt as a well-spring that is hidden from sight,
To the innermost heart of their own land they are known
As the stars are known to the Night;

As the stars that shall be bright when we are dust,
Moving in marches upon the heavenly plain;
As the stars that are starry in the time of our darkness,
To the end, to the end, they remain.

Laurence Binyon

August 1914

God said, 'Men have forgotten Me:
The souls that sleep shall wake again,
  And blinded eyes must learn to see.'

So since redemption comes through pain
He smote the earth with chastening rod,
  And brought destruction's lurid reign;

But where His desolation trod
The people in their agony
  Despairing cried, 'There is no God.'

Vera Brittain

Perhaps

Perhaps some day the sun will shine again,
    And I shall see that still the skies are blue,
And feel once more I do not live in vain,
Although bereft of You.

Perhaps the golden meadows at my feet
Will make the sunny hours of spring seem gay,
And I shall find the white May-blossoms sweet,
Though You have passed away.

Perhaps the summer woods will shimmer bright,
And crimson roses once again be fair,
And autumn harvest fields a rich delight,
Although You are not there.

Perhaps some day I shall not shrink in pain
To see the passing of the dying year,
And listen to Christmas songs again,
Although You cannot hear.

But though kind Time may many joys renew,
There is one greatest joy I shall not know
Again, because my heart for loss of You
Was broken, long ago.

Vera Brittain

To My Brother (In Memory of July 1st, 1916)

Your battle-wounds are scars upon my heart,
    Received when in that grand and tragic 'show'
You played your part
Two years ago,

And silver in the summer morning sun
I see the symbol of your courage glow –
That Cross you won
Two years ago,

Though now again you watch the shrapnel fly,
And hear the guns that daily louder grow,
As in July
Two years ago,

May you endure to lead the Last Advance
And with your men pursue the flying foe
As once in France
Two years ago.

Vera Brittain

Langemarck at Ypres

This is the ballad of Langemarck,
   A story of glory and might;
Of the vast Hun horde, and Canada's part
   In the great grim fight.

It was April fair on the Flanders Fields,
   But the dreadest April then
That ever the years, in their fateful flight,
   Had brought to this world of men.

North and east, a monster wall,
   The mighty Hun ranks lay,
With fort on fort, and iron-ringed trench,
   Menacing, grim and gray.

And south and west, like a serpent of fire,
   Serried the British lines,
And in between, the dying and dead,
And the stench of blood, and the trampled mud,
   On the fair, sweet Belgian vines.

And far to the eastward, harnessed and taut,
   Like a scimitar, shining and keen,
Gleaming out of that ominous gloom,
   Old France's hosts were seen.

When out of the grim Hun lines one night,
   There rolled a sinister smoke; –
A strange, weird cloud, like a pale, green shroud,
   And death lurked in its cloak.

On a fiend-like wind it curled along
   Over the brave French ranks,
Like a monster tree its vapours spread,
   In hideous, burning banks
Of poisonous fumes that scorched the night
   With their sulphurous demon danks.

And men went mad with horror, and fled
   From that terrible, strangling death,
That seemed to sear both body and soul
   With its baleful, flaming breath.

Till even the little dark men of the south,
   Who feared neither God nor man,
Those fierce, wild fighters of Afric's steppes,
   Broke their battalions and ran: –

Ran as they never had run before,
   Gasping, and fainting for breath;
For they knew 't was no human foe that slew;
   And that hideous smoke meant death.

Then red in the reek of that evil cloud,
   The Hun swept over the plain;
And the murderer's dirk did its monster work,
   'Mid the scythe-like shrapnel rain;

Till it seemed that at last the brute Hun hordes
  Had broken that wall of steel;
And that soon, through this breach in the freeman's dyke,
  His trampling hosts would wheel; —

And sweep to the south in ravaging might,
  And Europe's peoples again
Be trodden under the tyrant's heel,
  Like herds, in the Prussian pen.

But in that line on the British right,
  There massed a corps amain,
Of men who hailed from a far west land
  Of mountain and forest and plain;

Men new to war and its dreadest deeds,
  But noble and staunch and true;
Men of the open, East and West,
  Brew of old Britain's brew.

These were the men out there that night,
  When Hell loomed close ahead;
Who saw that pitiful, hideous rout,
  And breathed those gases dread;
While some went under and some went mad;
  But never a man there fled.

For the word was 'Canada', theirs to fight,
  And keep on fighting still; —
Britain said, fight, and fight they would,
Though the Devil himself in sulphurous mood
  Came over that hideous hill.

Yea, stubborn, they stood, that hero band,
  Where no soul hoped to live;
For five, 'gainst eighty thousand men,
  Were hopeless odds to give.

Yea, fought they on! 'T was Friday eve,
  When that demon gas drove down;
'T was Saturday eve that saw them still
  Grimly holding their own;

Sunday, Monday, saw them yet,
  A steadily lessening band,
With 'no surrender' in their hearts,
  But the dream of a far-off land,

Where mother and sister and love would weep
  For the hushed heart lying still; —
But never a thought but to do their part,
  And work the Empire's will.

Ringed round, hemmed in, and back to back,
  They fought there under the dark,
And won for Empire, God and Right,
  At grim, red Langemarck.

Wonderful battles have shaken this world,
  Since the Dawn-God overthrew Dis;
Wonderful struggles of right against wrong,
Sung in the rhymes of the world's great song,
  But never a greater than this.

Bannockburn, Inkerman, Balaclava,
  Marathon's godlike stand;
But never a more heroic deed,
And never a greater warrior breed,
  In any war-man's land.

This is the ballad of Langemarck,
  A story of glory and might;
Of the vast Hun horde, and Canada's part
  In the great, grim fight.

William Wilfred Campbell

Cambrai and Marne

Before our trenches at Cambrai
We saw their columns cringe away.
We saw their masses melt and reel
Before our line of leaping steel.

A handful to their storming hordes,
We scourged them with the scourge of swords,
And still, the more we slew, the more
Came up for every slain a score.

Between the hedges and the town
The cursing squadrons we rode down;
To stay them we outpoured our blood
Between the beetfields and the wood.

In that red hell of shrieking shell
Unfaltering our gunners fell;
They fell, or ere that day was done,
Beside the last unshattered gun.

But still we held them, like a wall
On which the breakers vainly fall—
Till came the word, and we obeyed,
Reluctant, bleeding, undismayed.
Our feet, astonished, learned retreat;
Our souls rejected still defeat;
Unbroken still, a lion at bay,
We drew back grimly from Cambrai.

In blood and sweat, with slaughter spent,
They thought us beaten as we went,
Till suddenly we turned, and smote
The shout of triumph in their throat.

At last, at last we turned and stood –
And Marne's fair water ran with blood;
We stood by trench and steel and gun,
For now the indignant flight was done.

We ploughed their shaken ranks with fire,
We trod their masses into mire;
Our sabres drove through their retreat
As drives the whirlwind through young wheat.

At last, at last we drove them back
Along their drenched and smoking track;
We hurled them back, in blood and flame,
The reeking ways by which they came.

By cumbered road and desperate ford
How fled their shamed and harassed horde!
Shout, Sons of Freemen, for the day
When Marne so well avenged Cambrai!

Charles G. D. Roberts

The Place of His Rest

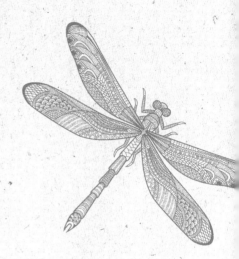

The green marsh-mallows
  Are over him.
Along the shallows
The pale lights swim.

Wide air, washed grasses,
And waveless stream;
And over him passes
The drift of dream; –

The pearl-hue down
Of the poplar seed;
The elm-flower brown;
And the sway of the reed;

The blue moth, winged
With a flake of sky;
The bee, gold ringed;
And the dragon fly.

Lightly the rushes
Lean to his breast;
A bird's wing brushes
The place of his rest.

The far-flown swallow,
The gold-finch flame, –
They come, they follow
The paths he came.

'Tis the land of No Care
Where now he lies,
Fulfilled the prayer
Of his weary eyes:

And while around him
The kind grass creeps.
Where peace hath found him
How sound he sleeps.

Well to his slumber
Attends the year:
Soft rains without number
Soft noons, blue clear.

With nights of balm,
And the dark, sweet hours
Brooding with calm,
Pregnant with flowers.

See how she speeds them,
Each childlike bloom,
And softly leads them
To tend his tomb! –

The white-thorn nears
As the cowslip goes;
Then the iris appears;
And then, the rose.

Charles G. D. Roberts

Visée/Aim

A Madame René Berthier

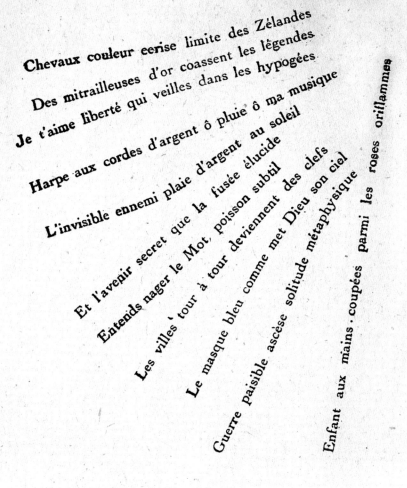

Chevaux couleur cerise limite des Zélandes

Des mitrailleuses d'or coassent les légendes

Je t'aime liberté qui veilles dans les hypogées

Harpe aux cordes d'argent ô pluie ô ma musique

L'invisible ennemi plaie d'argent au soleil

Et l'avenir secret que la fusée élucide

Entends nager le Mot, poisson subtil

Les villes tour à tour deviennent des clefs

Le masque bleu comme met Dieu son ciel

Guerre paisible ascèse solitude métaphysique

Enfant aux mains coupées parmi les roses oriflammes

(English translation)

To Madame René Berthier

Cherry coloured horses boundary of the Zealanders
Machine guns made of gold croak legends
I love you liberty who hide in basement rooms
Silver stringed hard O rain O my music
The invisible enemy a silver wound in the sun
And the secret future which the rocket illuminates
Listen to the Word, swim subtle fish
One by one the cities become keys
The blue mask just as God puts on his sky
Peaceable ascetic war metaphysical solitude
A child with its hands cut off among roses like flags

Apollinaire

Song of a Man Who has Come Through

Not I, not I, but the wind that blows through me!
A fine wind is blowing the new direction of Time.
If only I let it bear me, carry me, if only it carry me!
If only I am sensitive, subtle, oh, delicate, a winged gift!
If only, most lovely of all, I yield myself and am borrowed
By the fine, fine wind that takes its course though the
    chaos of the world
Like a fine, and exquisite chisel, a wedge-blade inserted;
If only I am keen and hard like the sheer tip of a wedge
Diven by invisible blows,
The rock will split, we shall come at the wonder, we shall
    find the Hesperides.

Oh, for the wonder that bubbles into my soul,
I would be a good fountain, a good well-head,
Would blur no whisper, spoil no expression.

What is the knocking?
What is the knocking at the door in the night?
It's somebody wants to do us harm.

No, no, it is the three strange angels.
Admit them, admit them.

D. H. Lawrence

War

To end the dreary day,
  The sun brought fire
And smote the grey
Of the heavens away
In his desire
That the evening sky might glow as red
As showed the earth with blood and ire.

The distant cannon's boom
In a land oppressed
Still spake the gloom
Of a country's doom,
Denying rest.
'War!' – called the frightened rooks and flew
From the crimson East to the crimson West.

Then, lest the dark might mar
The sky o'erhead,
There shone a star,
In the night afar
O'er each man's bed,
A symbol of undying peace,
The peace encompassing the dead.

Richard Dennys

Better Far to Pass Away

Better far to pass away
  While the limbs are strong and young,
Ere the ending of the day,
Ere youth's lusty song be sung.
Hot blood pulsing through the veins,
Youth's high hope a burning fire,
Young men needs must break the chains
That hold them from their hearts' desire.

My friends the hills, the sea, the sun,
The winds, the woods, the clouds, the trees –
How feebly, if my youth were done,
Could I, an old man, relish these!
With laughter, then, I'll go to greet
What Fate has still in store for me,
And welcome Death if we should meet,
And bear him willing company.

My share of fourscore years and ten
I'll gladly yield to any man,
And take no thought of 'where' or 'when,'
Contented with my shorter span,
For I have learned what love may be,
And found a heart that understands,
And known a comrade's constancy,
And felt the grip of friendly hands.

Come when it may, the stern decree
For me to leave the cheery throng
And quit the sturdy company
Of brothers that I work among.
No need for me to look askance,
Since no regret my prospect mars.
My day was happy – and perchance
The coming night is full of stars.

Richard Dennys

To a Lark in War-Time

Hail to thee, blithe spirit!
Bird thou never wert SHELLEY

Thou heavenly quivering beneath the deathlike above!
    Thou ethereal whirring above the deadly beneath!
Thou ever prolific, prolific soul!
Oh hope, not ours,
In the midst of this tearless abyss!
We lift our hardened feet
To drums and convicts' march.
Trumpets, whips on the open flesh
Flog us and force us ahead.

Still we can feel thee aloft
Over our slavish necks,
Thee, little ardent one,
Thee, God's flamelet of song.

Oh thou life, thou innocent speck,
Thou art not of us!
Because we lie,
We bellow and glare
When the guard herds us to soup.
We fear just one thing,
Our master, the whip.
And so we are not what we are.

But thou, tiny lark,
Thou unblemished, exquisite truth,
Thou doest thy life,
Thou livest thy song, and
Thou art what thou art.

Franz Werfel

Summer in England, 1914

On London fell a clearer light;
Caressing pencils of the sun
Defined the distances, the white
Houses transfigured one by one,
The 'long, unlovely street' impearled.
O what a sky has walked the world!

Most happy year! And out of town
The hay was prosperous, and the wheat;
The silken harvest climbed the down:
Moon after moon was heavenly-sweet,
Stroking the bread within the sheaves,
Looking 'twixt apples and their leaves.

And while this rose made round her cup,
The armies died convulsed. And when
This chaste young silver sun went up
Softly, a thousand shattered men,
One wet corruption, heaped the plain,
After a league-long throb of pain.

Flower following tender flower; and birds,
And berries; and benignant skies
Made thrive the serried flocks and herds. —
Yonder are men shot through the eyes.
Love, hide thy face
From man's unpardonable race.

Who said 'No man hath greater love than this,
To die to serve his friend'?
So these have loved us all unto the end.
Chide thou no more, O thou unsacrificed!
The soldier dying dies upon a kiss,
The very kiss of Christ.

Alice Meynell

The *Answer*

O the Tyrant Lord has drawn his sword,
And has flung the scabbard away.
He has said the word that loosed his horde
To ravage, destroy and slay.
'Then where are those who will dare oppose
The blast of my fury's flame?'
But a salty breeze swept across the seas,
And back the clear answer came:
'We have heard the boast of your mighty host,
And slaves will we ne'er become;
Let our deeds declare what our hearts will dare,
We come! We come! We come!'

J. M. Langstaff

The Little Coffin

Another victim carried to the grave
By sorrowing girl-children left to mourn –
Swept on to death by Kultur's cruel wave,
At tender age from life untimely torn!
A little baby there in coffin laid,
In waxen purity, in silence still –
The proud result of a triumphant raid,
Sent forth to gratify a tyrant's will!

A little baby, lying in its rest –
A little baby, pointing out the way –
(Torn from its grieving mother's bleeding breast),
For manhood to rise up – avenge the day
When it was there untimely robb'd of breath,
Sent thro' the valley dark by tyrant law –
A little baby lying there in death –
The Red Record has claim'd one victim more!

The girls tread softly, breathless with their grief,
Slow-pacing to the lonely churchyard sod,
Whilst bitter tears well up for their relief,
They slowly bear it there to rest in God.
And it shall lie there in its last long sleep,
Whilst still War's thunders roar above it's head –
And still the Red Record goes on to reap
Another victim, numbered with the dead.

Agnes Littlejohn

The Harvest Moon

Over the twilight field,
Over the glimmering field
And bleeding furrows, with their sodden yield
Of sheaves that still did writhe,
After the scythe;
The teeming field, and darkly overstrewn
With all the garnered fullness of that noon –
Two looked upon each other.
One was a Woman, men had called their mother:
And one the Harvest Moon.

And one the Harvest Moon
Who stood, who gazed
On those unquiet gleanings, where they bled;
Till the lone Woman said:

'But we were crazed...
We should laugh now together, I and you;
We two.
You, for your ever dreaming it was worth
A star's while to look on, and light the earth;
And I, for ever telling to my mind
Glory it was and gladness, to give birth
To human kind.
I gave the breath, – and thought it not amiss,
I gave the breath to men,
For men to slay again;
Lording it over anguish, all to give
My life, that men might live,
For this.

'You will be laughing now, remembering
We called you once Dead World, and barren thing.
Yes, so we called you then,
You, far more wise
Than to give life to men.'

Over the field that there
Gave back the skies
A scattered upward stare
From sightless eyes,
The furrowed field that lay
Striving awhile, through many a bleeding dune
Of throbbing clay, – but dumb and quiet soon,
She looked; and went her way,
The Harvest Moon.

Josephine Preston Peabody

A Kiss

She kissed me when she said good-bye –
A child's kiss, neither bold nor shy.

We had met but a few short summer hours;
Talked of the sun, the wind, the flowers,

Sports and people; had rambled through
A casual catchy song or two,

And walked with arms linked to the car
By the light of a single misty star.

(It was war-time, you see, and the streets
   were dark
Lest the ravishing Hun should find a mark.)

And so we turned to say good-bye;
But somehow or other, I don't know why,

– Perhaps 'twas the feel of the khaki coat
(She'd a brother in Flanders then) that smote

Her heart with a sudden tenderness
Which issued in that swift caress –

Somehow, to her, at any rate
A mere hand-clasp seemed inadequate;

And so she lifted her dewey face
And kissed me – but without a trace

Of passion, – and we said good-bye ...
A child's kiss, ... neither bold nor shy.

My friend, I like you – it seemed to say –
Here's to our meeting again some day!

Some happier day ...
Good-bye.

Bernard Freeman Trotter

Place de la Concorde

Near where the royal victims fell
In days gone by, caught in the swell
Of a ruthless tide
Of human passion, deep and wide:
There where we two
A Nation's later sorrow knew –
To-day, O friend! I stood
Amid a self-ruled multitude
That by nor sound nor word
Betrayed how mightily its heart was stirred.

A memory Time never could efface –
A memory of Grief –
Like a great Silence brooded o'er the place;
And men breathed hard, as seeking for relief
From an emotion strong
That would not cry, though held in check too long.

One felt that joy drew near –
A joy intense that seemed itself to fear –
Brightening in eyes that had been dull,
As all with feeling gazed
Upon the Strasbourg figure, raised
Above us – mourning, beautiful!

Then one stood at the statue's base, and spoke –
Men needed not to ask what word;
Each in his breast the message heard,
Writ for him by Despair,
That evermore in moving phrase
Breathes from the Invalides and Père Lachaise –

Vainly it seemed, alas!
But now, France looking on the image there,
Hope gave her back the lost Alsace.

A deeper hush fell on the crowd:
A sound – the lightest – seemed too loud
(Would, friend, you had been there!)
As to that form the speaker rose,
Took from her, fold on fold,
The mournful crape, gray-worn and old,
Her, proudly, to disclose,
And with the touch of tender care
That fond emotion speaks,
'Mid tears that none could quite command,
Placed the Tricolor in her hand,
And kissed her on both cheeks!

Florence Earle Coates

In War-Time / An American Homeward Bound

Further and further we leave the scene
  Of war – and of England's care;
I try to keep my mind serene –
  But my heart stays there;

For a distant song of pain and wrong
  My spirit doth deep confuse,
And I sit all day on the deck, and long –
  And long for news!

I seem to see them in battle-line –
  Heroes with hearts of gold,
But of their victory a sign
  The Fates withhold;

And the hours too tardy-footed pass,
  The voiceless hush grows dense
'Mid the imaginings, alas!
  That feed suspense.

Oh, might I lie on the wind, or fly
  In the wilful sea-bird's track,
Would I hurry on, with a homesick cry –
  Or hasten back?

Florence Earle Coates

In Flanders Fields

In Flanders fields the poppies blow
Between the crosses, row on row,
That mark our place; and in the sky
The larks, still bravely singing, fly
Scarce heard amid the guns below.

We are the Dead. Short days ago,
We lived, felt dawn, saw sunset glow,
Loved and were loved, and now we lie
     In Flanders fields.

Take up our quarrel with the foe:
To you from failing hands we throw
The torch; be yours to hold it high.
If ye break faith with us who die
We shall not sleep, though poppies grow
     In Flanders fields.

John McCrae

The Unconquered Dead

'... defeated, with great loss.'

Not we the conquered! Not to us the blame
   Of them that flee, of them that basely yield;
Nor ours the shout of victory, the fame
   Of them that vanquish in a stricken field.

That day of battle in the dusty heat
   We lay and heard the bullets swish and sing
Like scythes amid the over-ripened wheat,
   And we the harvest of their garnering.

Some yielded, No, not we! Not we, we swear
   By these our wounds; this trench upon the hill
Where all the shell-strewn earth is seamed and bare,
   Was ours to keep; and lo! we have it still.

We might have yielded, even we, but death
  Came for our helper; like a sudden flood
The crashing darkness fell; our painful breath
  We drew with gasps amid the choking blood.

The roar fell faint and farther off, and soon
  Sank to a foolish humming in our ears,
Like crickets in the long, hot afternoon
  Among the wheat fields of the olden years.

Before our eyes a boundless wall of red
  Shot through by sudden streaks of jagged pain!
Then a slow-gathering darkness overhead
  And rest came on us like a quiet rain.

Not we the conquered! Not to us the shame,
  Who hold our earthen ramparts, nor shall cease
To hold them ever; victors we, who came
  In that fierce moment to our honoured peace.

John McCrae

The Anxious Dead

O guns, fall silent till the dead men hear
    Above their heads the legions pressing on:
(These fought their fight in time of bitter fear,
    And died not knowing how the day had gone.)

O flashing muzzles, pause, and let them see
    The coming dawn that streaks the sky afar;
Then let your mighty chorus witness be
    To them, and Caesar, that we still make war.

Tell them, O guns, that we have heard their call,
    That we have sworn, and will not turn aside,
That we will onward till we win or fall,
    That we will keep the faith for which they died.

Bid them be patient, and some day, anon,
    They shall feel earth enwrapt in silence deep;
Shall greet, in wonderment, the quiet dawn,
    And in content may turn them to their sleep.

John McCrae

140

On Receiving News of War

Snow is a strange word;
No ice or frost
Have asked of bud or bird
For Winter's cost.

Yet ice and frost and snow
From earth to sky
This Summer land doth know,
No man knows why.

In all men's hearts it is.
Some spirit old
Hath turned with malign kiss
Our lives to mould.

Red fangs have torn His face.
God's blood is shed.
He mourns from His lone place
His children dead.

O! ancient crimson curse!
Corrode, consume.
Give back this universe
Its pristine bloom.

Isaac Rosenberg

Break of Day in the Trenches

The darkness crumbles away.
  It is the same old druid Time as ever,
Only a live thing leaps my hand,
A queer sardonic rat,
As I pull the parapet's poppy
To stick behind my ear.
Droll rat, they would shoot you if they knew
Your cosmopolitan sympathies.
Now you have touched this English hand
You will do the same to a German
Soon, no doubt, if it be your pleasure
To cross the sleeping green between.
It seems you inwardly grin as you pass
Strong eyes, fine limbs, haughty athletes,
Less chanced than you for life,
Bonds to the whims of murder,
Sprawled in the bowels of the earth,
The torn fields of France.
What do you see in our eyes
At the shrieking iron and flame
Hurled through still heavens?
What quaver – what heart aghast?
Poppies whose roots are in man's veins
Drop, and are ever dropping;
But mine in my ear is safe –
Just a little white with the dust.

Isaac Rosenberg

Dead Man's Dump

The plunging limbers over the shattered track
    Racketed with their rusty freight,
Stuck out like many crowns of thorns,
And the rusty stakes like sceptres old
To stay the flood of brutish men
Upon our brothers dear.

The wheels lurched over sprawled dead
But pained them not, though their bones crunched,
Their shut mouths made no moan.
They lie there huddled, friend and foeman,
Man born of man, and born of woman,
And shells go crying over them
From night till night and now.

Earth has waited for them,
All the time of their growth
Fretting for their decay:
Now she has them at last!
In the strength of their strength
Suspended – stopped and held.

What fierce imaginings their dark souls lit?
Earth! have they gone into you!
Somewhere they must have gone,
And flung on your hard back
Is their soul's sack,
Emptied of God-ancestralled essences.
Who hurled them out? Who hurled?

None saw their spirits' shadow shake the grass,
Or stood aside for the half-used life to pass
Out of those doomed nostrils and the doomed mouth,
When the swift iron burning bee
Drained the wild honey of their youth.

What of us who, flung on the shrieking pyre,
Walk, our usual thoughts untouched,
Our lucky limbs as on ichor fed,
Immortal seeming ever?
Perhaps when the flames beat loud on us,
A fear may choke in our veins
And the startled blood may stop.

The air is loud with death,
The dark air spurts with fire,
The explosions ceaseless are.

Timelessly now, some minutes past,
These dead strode time with vigorous life,
Till the shrapnel called 'An end!'
But not to all. In bleeding pangs
Some borne on stretchers dreamed of home,
Dear things, war-blotted from their hearts.

A man's brains splattered on
A stretcher-bearer's face;
His shook shoulders slipped their load,
But when they bent to look again
The drowning soul was sunk too deep
For human tenderness.

They left this dead with the older dead,
Stretched at the cross roads.
Burnt black by strange decay
Their sinister faces lie
The lid over each eye,
The grass and coloured clay
More motion have than they,
Joined to the great sunk silences.

Here is one not long dead;
His dark hearing caught our far wheels,
And the choked soul stretched weak hands
To reach the living word the far wheels said,
The blood-dazed intelligence beating for light,
Crying through the suspense of the far torturing wheels
Swift for the end to break
Or the wheels to break,
Cried as the tide of the world broke over his sight.

Will they come? Will they ever come?
Even as the mixed hoofs of the mules,
The quivering-bellied mules,
And the rushing wheels all mixed
With his tortured upturned sight,
So we crashed round the bend,
We heard his weak scream,
We heard his very last sound,
And our wheels grazed his dead face.

Isaac Rosenberg

Girl to a Soldier on Leave

I love you – Titan lover,
My own storm-days' Titan.
Greater than the son of Zeus,
I know whom I would choose.

Titan – my splendid rebel –
The old Prometheus
Wanes like a ghost before your power –
His pangs were joys to yours.

Pallid days arid and wan
Tied your soul fast.
Babel-cities' smoky tops
Pressed upon your growth

Weary gyves. What were you
But a word in the brain's ways,
Or the sleep of Circe's swine.
One gyve holds you yet. –

It held you hiddenly on the Somme
Tied from my heart at home.
O must it loosen now? – I wish
You were bound with the old gyves.

Love! you love me – your eyes
Have looked through death at mine.
You have tempted a grave too much.
I let you – I repine.

Isaac Rosenberg

Futility

Move him into the sun –
Gently its touch awoke him once,
At home, whispering of fields unsown.
Always it woke him, even in France,
Until this morning and this snow.
If anything might rouse him now
The kind old sun will know.

Think how it wakes the seeds, –
Woke, once the clays of a cold star.
Are limbs, so dear-achieved, are sides
Full-nerved, – still warm, – too hard to stir?
Was it for this the clay grew tall?
– O what made fatuous sunbeams toil
To break earth's sleep at all?

Wilfred Owen

Spring Offensive

Halted against the shade of a last hill,
They fed, and, lying easy, were at ease
And, finding comfortable chest and knees
Carelessly slept. But many there stood still
To face the stark, blank sky beyond the ridge,
Knowing their feet had come to the end of the world.

Marvelling they stood, and watched the long grass swirled
By the May breeze, murmurous with wasp and midge,
For though the summer oozed into their veins
Like the injected drug for their bodies' pains,
Sharp on their souls hung the imminent line of grass,
Fearfully flashed the sky's mysterious glass.

Hour after hour they ponder the warm field, –
And the far valley behind, where the buttercups
Had blessed with gold their slow boots coming up,
Where even the little brambles would not yield,
But clutched and clung to them like sorrowing hands;
They breathe like trees unstirred.

Till like a cold gust thrilled the little word
At which each body and its soul begird
And tighten them for battle. No alarms
Of bugles, no high flags, no clamorous haste, –
Only a lift and flare of eyes that faced
The sun, like a friend with whom their love is done.
O larger shone that smile against the sun, –
Mightier than his whose bounty these have spurned.

So, soon they topped the hill, and raced together
Over an open stretch of herb and heather
Exposed. And instantly the whole sky burned
With fury against them; earth set sudden cups
In thousands for their blood; and the green slope
Chasmed and steepened sheer to infinite space.

Of them who running on that last high place
Leapt to swift unseen bullets, or went up
On the hot blast and fury of hell's upsurge,
Or plunged and fell away past this world's verge,
Some say God caught them even before they fell.

But what say such as from existence' brink
Ventured but drave too swift to sink,
The few who rushed in the body to enter hell,
And there out-fiending all its fiends and flames
With superhuman inhumanities,
Long-famous glories, immemorial shames –
And crawling slowly back, have by degrees
Regained cool peaceful air in wonder –
Why speak not they of comrades that went under?

Wilfred Owen

Smile, Smile, Smile

Head to limp head, the sunk-eyed wounded scanned
Yesterday's *Mail*; the casualties (typed small)
And (large) Vast Booty from our Latest Haul.
Also, they read of Cheap Homes, not yet planned,
'For', said the paper, 'when this war is done
The men's first instinct will be making homes.
Meanwhile their foremost need is aerodromes,
It being certain war has but begun.
Peace would do wrong to our undying dead, –
The sons we offered might regret they died
If we got nothing lasting in their stead.
We must be solidly indemnified.
Though all be worthy Victory which all bought.
We rulers sitting in this ancient spot
Would wrong our very selves if we forgot
The greatest glory will be theirs who fought,
Who kept this nation in integrity.'
Nation? – The half-limbed readers did not chafe
But smiled at one another curiously
Like secret men who know their secret safe.
(This is the thing they know and never speak,
That England one by one had fled to France
Not many elsewhere now, save under France.)
Pictures of these broad smiles appear each week,
And people in whose voice real feeling rings
Say: How they smile! They're happy now, poor things.

Wilfred Owen

Anthem for a Doomed Youth

What passing-bells for these who die as cattle?
    – Only the monstrous anger of the guns.
Only the stuttering rifles' rapid rattle
Can patter out their hasty orisons.
No mockeries now for them; no prayers nor bells;
Nor any voice of mourning save the choirs, –
The shrill, demented choirs of wailing shells;
And bugles calling for them from sad shires.

What candles may be held to speed them all?
Not in the hands of boys, but in their eyes
Shall shine the holy glimmers of goodbyes.
The pallor of girls' brows shall be their pall;
Their flowers the tenderness of patient minds,
And each slow dusk a drawing-down of blinds.

Wilfred Owen

Strange Meeting

It seemed that out of battle I escaped
Down some profound dull tunnel, long since scooped
Through granites which titanic wars had groined.

Yet also there encumbered sleepers groaned,
Too fast in thought or death to be bestirred.
Then, as I probed them, one sprang up, and stared
With piteous recognition in fixed eyes,
Lifting distressful hands, as if to bless.
And by his smile, I knew that sullen hall, –
By his dead smile I knew we stood in Hell.

With a thousand fears that vision's face was grained;
Yet no blood reached there from the upper ground,
And no guns thumped, or down the flues made moan.
'Strange friend', I said, 'here is no cause to mourn.'
'None', said that other, 'save the undone years,
The hopelessness. Whatever hope is yours,
Was my life also; I went hunting wild
After the wildest beauty in the world,
Which lies not calm in eyes, or braided hair,
But mocks the steady running of the hour,
And if it grieves, grieves richlier than here.
For by my glee might many men have laughed,
And of my weeping something had been left,
Which must die now. I mean the truth untold,
The pity of war, the pity war distilled.
Now men will go content with what we spoiled,
Or, discontent, boil bloody, and be spilled.

They will be swift with swiftness of the tigress.
None will break ranks, though nations trek from progress.
Courage was mine, and I had mystery;
Wisdom was mine, and I had mastery:
To miss the march of this retreating world
Into vain citadels that are not walled.
Then, when much blood had clogged their chariot-wheels,
I would go up and wash them from sweet wells,
Even with truths that lie too deep for taint.
I would have poured my spirit without stint
But not through wounds; not on the cess of war.
Foreheads of men have bled where no wounds were.

'I am the enemy you killed, my friend.
I knew you in this dark: for so you frowned
Yesterday through me as you jabbed and killed.
I parried; but my hands were loath and cold.
Let us sleep now. . . .'

Wilfred Owen

Soldiers from the Wars Returning

Soldier from the wars returning,
Spoiler of the taken town,
Here is ease that asks not earning;
Turn you in and sit you down.

Peace is come and wars are over,
Welcome you and welcome all,
While the charger crops the clover
And his bridle hangs in stall.

Now no more of winters biting,
Filth in trench from tall to spring,
Summers full of sweat and fighting
For the Kesar or the King.

Rest you, charger, rust you, bridle;
Kings and kesars, keep your pay;
Soldier, sit you down and idle
At the inn of night for aye.

A. E. Housman

The Cenotaph

Not yet will those measureless fields be green again
Where only yesterday the wild sweet blood of
wonderful youth was shed;
There is a grave whose earth must hold too long, too
deep a stain,
Though for ever over it we may speak as proudly as we
may tread.

But here, where the watchers by lonely hearths from the
     thrust of an inward sword have more slowly bled,
We shall build the Cenotaph: Victory, winged, with Peace,
     winged too, at the column's head.
And over the stairway, at the foot – oh! here, leave
     desolate, passionate hands to spread
Violets, roses, and laurel with the small sweet twinkling
     country things
Speaking so wistfully of other Springs
From the little gardens of little places where son or
     sweetheart was born and bred.
In splendid sleep, with a thousand brothers
     To lovers – to mothers
     Here, too, lies he:
Under the purple, the green, the red,
It is all young life: it must break some women's hearts to see
Such a brave, gay coverlet to such a bed!
Only, when all is done and said,
God is not mocked and neither are the dead.
For this will stand in our Market-place –
     Who'll sell, who'll buy
     (Will you or I
Lie each to each with the better grace)?
While looking into every busy whore's and huckster's face
As they drive their bargains, is the Face
Of God: and some young, piteous, murdered face.

Charlotte Mew

Biographies

GUILLAUME APOLLINAIRE (1890–1918): Born in Rome and of Polish descent, he was a poet, playwright, writer, novelist and art critic. He influenced the development of Cubism, Dadaism, Futurism and Surrealism. In 1914, he joined the French Army and was wounded in 1916.

ARTHUR HENRY ADAMS (1872–1936): Born in New Zealand, he initially studied law and then became a journalist contributing to various newspapers. He was also a novelist and playwright.

LAURENCE BINYON (1869–1943): Born in Lancashire, he was a poet, art scholar and dramatist. Educated at Oxford University, he won the Newdigate Prize for Poetry and worked in the British Museum for 40 years.

VERA BRITTAIN (1893–1970): Born in Newcastle, Vera Brittain was educated at Oxford. She worked as a Voluntary Aid Detachment nurse during World War I in England, France and Malta. She suffered from her experiences in the war and became an influential pacifist, regularly speaking on behalf of the League of Nations.

RUPERT BROOKE (1887–1915): Born in Warwickshire, Brooke was a graduate of Cambridge University, and was a familiar figure in literary and political circles. He entered the war as a sub-lieutenant in the Royal Naval Division. While sailing the Aegean on the way to Gallipoli, he died of acute blood poisoning, the result of a mosquito bite.

WILLIAM WILFRED CAMPBELL (1860–1918): Born in Ontario, he is classed as one of Canada's Confederation Poets.

FLORENCE EARLE COATES (1850–1927): Born in Pennsylvania, she became well known in America and abroad for her poetry, and in 1915, she was elected poet laureate of Pennsylvania by the state's Federation of Women's Clubs.

RICHARD DENNYS (1884–1916): Born in London, Dennys was first schooled in medicine, and then pursued a career in the arts. He was mortally wounded at the Battle of the Somme.

LENA GILBERT FORD (1870–1918): Born in Pennsylvania, she was a lyricist. She moved to England where she met Ivor Novello, with whom she collaborated to produce 'Keep The Home Fires Burning'.

FORD MADOX FORD (1873–1939): Born in Surrey, he was an English novelist, poet, art critic and editor. He was the grandson of the Pre-Raphaelite painter Ford Madox Brown.

JULIAN GRENFELL (1888–1915): The eldest son of the Earl of Desborough, he was born in London. He joined the Royal Dragoons and was hit by shrapnel during the Second Battle of Ypres. He died four weeks later.

IVOR GURNEY (1890–1937): Born in Gloucester, he was a poet and composer. He enlisted in 1915 as a private soldier in the Gloucester Regiment. He was wounded and gassed. During his life, he suffered from mental health issues and spent time in psychiatric hospitals.

THOMAS HARDY (1840-1928): Born in Dorset, Hardy is one of the most renowned poets and novelists in English literature.

W. N. HODGSON (1893–1916): The son of a bishop, Hodgson was born in Gloucestershire. After being sent to France, he became a popular writer. He was killed by machine-gun fire near Mametz.

A. E. HOUSMAN (1859–1936): Born in Worcestershire, he was a classical scholar and poet, best known for the cycle of poems *A Shropshire Lad*.

T. E. HULME (1883–1917): Born in Staffordshire, he was a poet and philosopher, best known for his leadership of the group the 'imagists'. His was a major influence on art and literature.

T. M. KETTLE (1880–1916): Born in Dublin, he was a journalist, poet, barrister and Home Rule politician. Kettle enlisted in the British Army in 1914, and was killed in action in 1916.

JOYCE KILMER (1886–1918): Born in New Jersey, he graduated from Columbia University. He was an editor, journalist and poet. He enlisted in 1917, after the United States entered the war. He was shot by a sniper outside Ourcq, France.

RUDYARD KIPLING (1865–1936): Born in Bombay, he was educated in England. His only son was killed in the Battle of the Loos in September, 1915. He is best known for his children's books. In 1907, he was awarded the Nobel Price for Literature.

J. M. LANGSTAFF (1883–1917): Born in Ontario, he studied law in Toronto. His academic achievements were matched by his military record and he achieved the rank of major. He was killed at the Battle of Vimy Ridge.

D. H. LAWRENCE (1885–1930): Born in Nottinghamshire, he was a novelist, poet, playwright, literay critic and painter.

AMY LOWELL (1874–1925): Born in Massachusetts, she was an American poet of the 'imagist' school. Lowell posthumously won the Pulitzer Prize for Poetry in 1926.

E. ALAN MACKINTOSH (1893–1917): Born in Brighton and educated at Oxford University, he enlisted with the 5th Seaforth Highlanders at the end of 1914. He served in France from July 1915 and was killed on the second day of the Battle of Cambrai in 1917.

JOHN McCRAE (1872–1918): Born in Ontario, he studied medicine at the University of Toronto. McCrae served in the Boer War and as a lieutenant-colonel, and in World War I as a surgeon at a hospital in Boulogne, where he died.

CHARLOTTE MEW (1869–1928): Born in London, she was a writer and poet. Her life was full of tragedy and themes of death and loss fill her poems.

ALICE MEYNELL (1847–1922): Born in London, she was brought up in Italy. She was a writer, editor, critic, poet and suffragist.

SIR HENRY NEWBOLT (1862–1932): Born in Wolverhampton, he was a novelist, historian and poet. He was a government advisor, particularly on Irish issues.

ROBERT NICHOLS (1893–1944): Educated at Oxford University, he was a writer and playwright, best known as a war poet during World War I. He served in the Royal Artillery as an officer in 1914. He was invalided in 1916.

WILFRED OWEN (1893–1918): Born in Shropshire, he enlisted in 1915 and in May 1917, while serving in the trenches in France, he was caught in an explosion. Diagnosed with shellshock, he was sent to England to recover. He returned to France in 1918, and was awarded the Military Cross soon after. He was killed by German machine-gun fire in 1918.

JOSEPHINE PRESTON PEABODY (1874–1922): Born in New York, she was a teacher, poet and dramatist.

COLWYN PHILIPPS (1888–1915): The eldest son of the First Baron of St. David's, he was born in London. He served as a captain in the Royal Horse Guards until his death during the Second Battle of Ypres.

MARJORIE PICKTHALL (1883–1922): Born in England, her family then moved to Toronto, where she grew up. She was a poet, novelist and illustrator who considered one of Canada's finest poets in the 1920s.

JESSIE POPE (1868-1941): Born in Leicester, she was educated at the North London Collegiate School for Girls. Pope was a prolific writer, well known for her patriotic verses she wrote during World War I.

CHARLES D. G. ROBERTS (1860–1943): Born in New Brunswick, he is considered the 'Father of Canadian Poetry'. He published numerous works on exploration, natural history, travel and fiction.

ISAAC ROSENBERG (1890–1918): Born in Bristol to Russian immigrants, he considered himself a portrait artist rather than a poet. He was killed in close combat near the French village of Fampoux.

SIEGFRIED SASSOON (1886–1967): Born in Kent, he was educated at Cambridge University. Sassoon was the first war poet to volunteer in 1914. He was captain of the Royal Welch Fusiliers and won a Military Cross.

OWEN SEAMAN (1861–1936): Born in Shrewsbury, he was educated at Cambridge and was a poet, journalist and poet, best known as the editor of *Punch* from 1906 to 1932.

ALAN SEEGER (1888–1916): Born in New York, he spent much of his childhood in Mexico. Educated at Harvard, Seeger joined the French Foreign Legion and was killed in France at Belloy-en-Santerre.

MAY SINCLAIR (1863–1946): Born in Cheshire, she as an active feminist, novelist and writer. She was a suffragist and member of the Women Writers' Suffrage League

CHARLES HAMILTON SORLEY (1895–1915): Born in Aberdeen, he won a scholarship to Oxford University, but chose to defer entry to enlist in 1914. He was commissioned as a captain and was killed by a sniper at the Battle of Loos.

EDWARD THOMAS (1878–1917): Born in London to Welsh parents, he studied at Oxford University. In 1899, he married the daughter of James Ashcroft Noble and encouraged by his father-in-law, he pursued a life in letters as an author, editor and reviewer. He was killed by a shell at Arras.

BERNARD FREEMAN TROTTER (1890–1917) Born in Toronto, he spent much of his youth in Nova Scotia. He enlisted in March 1916 and, while serving as a Transport Officer at the Front in 1917, he was killed by a shell.

KATHARINE TYNAN (1859–1931): Born in County Dublin, Tynan was a novelist and poet, and a close associate of William Butler Yeats.

ARTHUR GRAEME WEST (1891–1917): Born in Norfolk, he spent his childhood in London, was educated at Oxford University and enlisted as a private in 1915. West quickly rose to the rank of captain before being killed by a sniper outside Bapaume, France.

FRANZ WERFEL (1890–1945): Born in Prague, he served in the Austro-Hungarian Army on the Russian Front as a telephone operator. Werfel was a novelist, playwright and poet.

EDITH WHARTON (1862–1937): Born in New York City, she was a Pulitzer Price-winning American novelist, short story writer and designer.

ELLA WHEELER WILCOX (1850–1919): Born in Wisconsin, her poetry was being published by the time she graduated from high school.

WILLIAM BUTLER YEATS (1865–1939): Born in Sandymount, Ireland, he was an Irish poet and one of the foremost figures of twentieth-century literature. In 1923, Yeats was awarded the Nobel Prize for Literature.